Word 2000
Made Simple

Keith Brindley

MADE SIMPLE
BOOKS

OXFORD AUCKLAND BOSTON JOHANNESBURG MELBOURNE NEW DELHI

652

HO ,101 238550X

Made Simple
An imprint of Butterworth-Heinemann
Linacre House, Jordan Hill, Oxford OX2 8DP
225 Wildwood Avenue, Woburn, MA 01801-2041
A division of Reed Educational and Professional Publishing Ltd

 A member of the Reed Elsevier plc group

First published 2000
© Keith Brindley 2000

TRADEMARKS/REGISTERED TRADEMARKS
Computer hardware and software brand names mentioned in this
book are protected by their respective trademarks and are acknowledged

British Library Cataloguing in Publication Data
A catalogue record for this book is available from the British Library

ISBN 0 7506 4181 9

 Typeset and produced by Co-publications, Loughborough
All screenshots taken with Screen Thief for Windows from Nildram Software (info@nildram.co.uk)
Icons designed by Sarah Ward © 1994
Printed and bound in Great Britain

FOR EVERY TITLE THAT WE PUBLISH, BUTTERWORTH-HEINEMANN
WILL PAY FOR BTCV TO PLANT AND CARE FOR A TREE.

Contents

Contents (contd)

Preface

Learning something new is never easy.

From our first faltering steps to passing exams; from riding a bike to driving a car; life is about acquiring new knowledge and ability — and all of this takes time and effort.

Thing is, a computer is probably the hardest of all to learn. Oh yes, if you fall off it on a bad bend you don't graze your knee, and you don't need comprehensive insurance for when it crashes, but it's hard nevertheless. A computer represents the ultimate in human technical achievement. The computer age is the culmination of the iron age, the bronze age, the industrial age — *all* the ages rolled into one. In a single box, the computer represents *everything* that humankind has ever done before…

…OK, so I'm getting carried away a little. A computer is, after all, just a machine. But it's a machine controlled in a different way to other machines. With a bike you turn the pedals, keep the handlebars roughly level and you're away, aren't you? Driving a car's merely a question of pressing a combination of pedals in the right order, moving a couple of sticks around at the right times, and turning a round thing to keep the whole thing on the road, right?

And computing's just a matter of pressing a few keys and dragging a plastic brick around the table, isn't it?

Of course not! Computing's all about being able to use its computer programs to do various jobs. Word 2000 is just a computer program — albeit a fairly complicated one. And the best way to learn it; indeed, the best way to learn any new complicated task — walking, cycling car driving included — is to break it down into manageable chunks.

That's what this book aims to do. Each task is shown step-by-step in an easy-to-follow format. Together, the tasks will give

contd…

you a good working knowledge of Word 2000, and — hopefully — the confidence to use it to your advantage.

Tasks included in this books begin at the very simplest — from first starting Word 2000, through saving of files, editing of documents, ways of changing your viewpoint of documents. On the other hand, more complex tasks are described too — ways to format and control text, styles, sections, margins, headers and footers, tables, borders, graphics and so on. In other words, it's the ideal accompaniment for the relatively new user — whether you're new just to Word 2000, or new to a computer altogether.

However, if you wish to do even more complex office-based tasks (such as; mail merges, macros, tables of contents, indexes and so on) you'll find this sort of information included in the Word 2000 Business Edition (ISBN 0750646101).

1   The basics

Starting up

First operation you ever do when using Word is to start it up.
Use the **Start** button, and access its sub-menu.

Basic steps:

1 Click the **Start** button

2 Point to the **Programs** menu entry – a sub-menu entry pops out

3 Point to then click the **Microsoft Word** sub-menu entry (if you have Microsoft Office installed on your computer, you'll first have to point to the **MSOffice** sub-menu entry – which will create a further pop-out menu to locate the **Microsoft Word** sub-menu entry)

2 Point to the **Programs** menu entry (you don't need to click)

3 Point to and click **Microsoft Word**

1 Click the **Start** button

After starting, you'll see the main Word window (shown right — for a completely new and unaltered program). If your copy of Word has been adapted by any other user since installation your screen may display something a little different.

Take note:

This whole process of clicking the **Start** button (or a menu) and navigating to your required sub-menu entry is abbreviated from now on in this book as a statement such as:

    choose Start↪Microsoft Word,

or:

    choose Tools↪Word Count

Tip:

If you use your computer only for word processing, you can set up to run Word each time you turn on your machine — see page 144 for details

Main features of a Word document window are shown below, but don't panic — they'll be looked at shortly. Soon you'll think Word is one of the easiest computer programs to get the hang of — and you'll be right.

The Word menu bar leads to commands available

Toolbars feature easily-clickable buttons which allow you to choose commands quickly

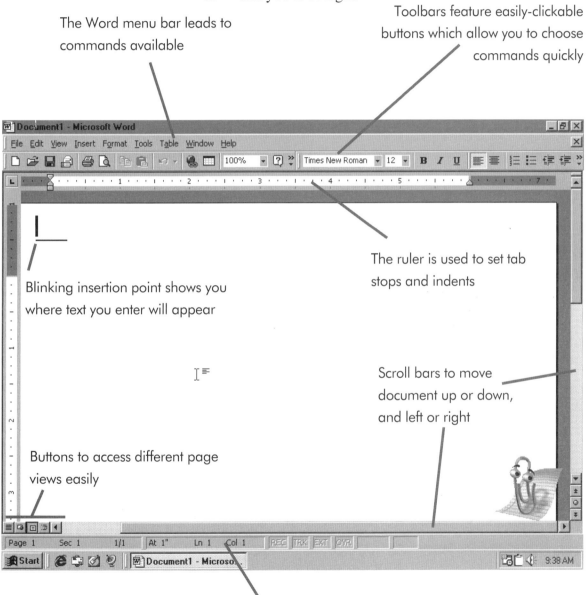

The ruler is used to set tab stops and indents

Blinking insertion point shows you where text you enter will appear

Scroll bars to move document up or down, and left or right

Buttons to access different page views easily

The status bar along the bottom gives details about the document in the window (see pages 28—29 for more details)

Word menus

Word has nine menus in its menu bar. They hold all the commands and tools available to any user of Word. While you don't (and that's just as well!) need to know what all these commands and tools are to get good results from Word, it's worth looking at all the menus to get an overall feel for what they are about — use this page as a reference.

The menu bar itself looks like this:

Basic steps:

1 To display a menu, click its name in the menu bar

2 Alternatively, enter [Alt] + the menu's underlined letter

3 To remove a displayed menu, click anywhere else in the window

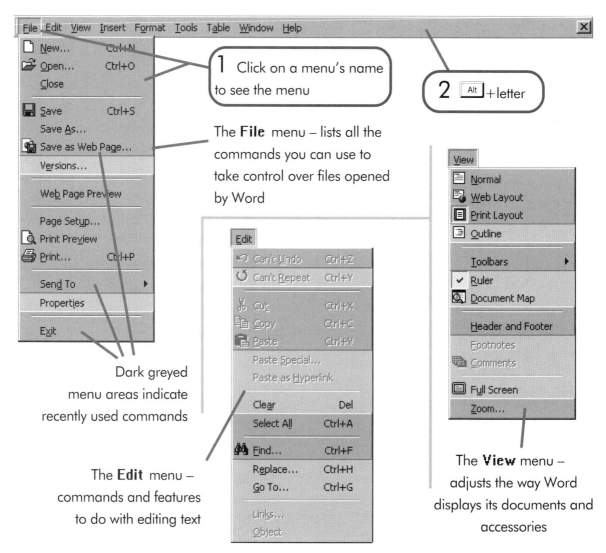

1 Click on a menu's name to see the menu

2 [Alt] + letter

The **File** menu – lists all the commands you can use to take control over files opened by Word

Dark greyed menu areas indicate recently used commands

The **Edit** menu – commands and features to do with editing text

The **View** menu – adjusts the way Word displays its documents and accessories

4

The **Insert** menu – used to place certain features over and above ordinary text into a document

The **Tools** menu – special features and controls

The **Table** menu – controls aspects of tables within a document

The **Format** menu – the menu you use to apply styles and so on to your document

The **Help** menu – how to how to?

The **Window** menu – choose between documents and control how they are displayed

5

Help me, I'm drowning!

Inevitably you will find there are times you don't know what you are doing. This happens whenever you are new (and, sometimes not-so-new) to a complex program like Word. Fortunately, Word has an incredibly useful — and even-more-incredibly comprehensive — on-line help system built-in to it. This comes in three parts:

● first there are ScreenTips — little labels which show up (1) when you point over any of the myriad buttons Word has in its many toolbars, and (2) at other specific places

● second is the Office Assistant — a sort of electronic dogs-body that monitors where you are within Word, and gives contextual help and advice if you need

● third is Help — an easily accessible system in which you can locate help about any feature, command or topic in Word.

SCREENTIPS

1 Simply position your pointer over any button in any toolbar to see the button's name as a label

OFFICE ASSISTANT

2 If not already displayed, click the Office Assistant button ⟨?⟩ on the Standard toolbar, choose **Help→Microsoft Word Help**, type ⟨Alt⟩+⟨H⟩ then ⟨H⟩, or (best) type ⟨F1⟩. Once displayed, as you move around within Word, the Office Assistant will provide help

3 Type in a word or phrase describing what you'd like help about

> **1** ScreenTips give each button a name as the pointer passes over it

> **What would you like to do?**
> Type your question here, and then click Search.
> Options   Search

> **2** The Office Assistant – always there to lend a (slightly tacky) hand

Take note:

If you want, turn off ScreenTips by unchecking the Show ScreenTips on tool-bars check box on the Options tab of the Customize dialog box (see page 9)

4 Click **Search**, or type `Alt` + `F`

5 In the resultant list of topics the Office Assistant displays about your request (assuming it has found something in its database that matches), click the topic you want

6 The **Word Help** window is displayed, listing sub-topics of the topic you asked for. Click the sub-topic you want

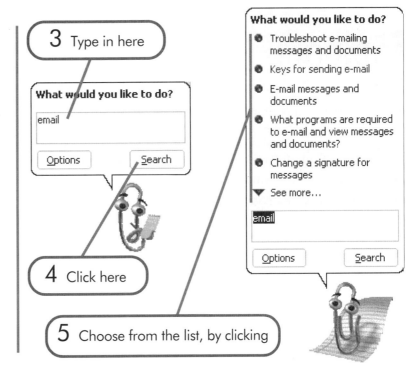

3 Type in here

What would you like to do?

email

Options   Search

4 Click here

5 Choose from the list, by clicking

What would you like to do?
- Troubleshoot e-mailing messages and documents
- Keys for sending e-mail
- E-mail messages and documents
- What programs are required to e-mail and view messages and documents?
- Change a signature for messages
- See more...

email

Options   Search

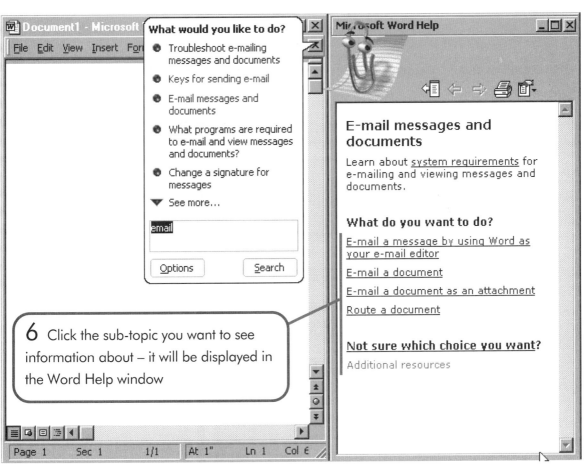

6 Click the sub-topic you want to see information about – it will be displayed in the Word Help window

E-mail messages and documents

Learn about system requirements for e-mailing and viewing messages and documents.

What do you want to do?

E-mail a message by using Word as your e-mail editor

E-mail a document

E-mail a document as an attachment

Route a document

Not sure which choice you want?

Additional resources

Toolbars

Apart from choosing commands in menus, Word is controlled by on-screen buttons, found in toolbars. The two most obvious toolbars are at the top of a Word document but, as we'll see, there are others, too — and further — Word lets you customize them to your heart's content — see page 146 for more details.

see page 146 for more details.

1 To display any particular toolbar, choose **View ↳ Toolbars**

2 In the **Toolbars** pop-out menu, drag to the toolbar you want displayed, then click

The standard toolbar – buttons used for common everyday tasks

This symbol indicates there are more buttons – click to see them

The default toolbar is split into two halves – the standard toolbar and the formatting toolbar

The formatting toolbar – containing buttons you use to stylise text within documents

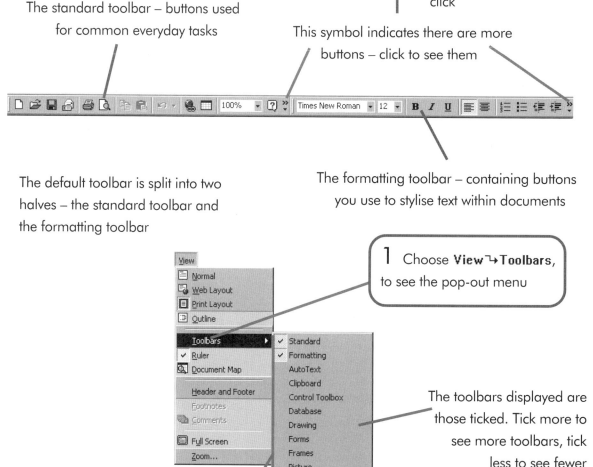

1 Choose **View ↳ Toolbars**, to see the pop-out menu

The toolbars displayed are those ticked. Tick more to see more toolbars, tick less to see fewer

2 Drag in the pop-out menu to the toolbar you want displayed (or to be removed!), then click

8

3 Alternatively, use the mouse shortcut – click any toolbar with the right mouse button

4 Click the toolbar you want turned on or off

You can turn off any existing toolbar, or turn on any of the other toolbars (see previous page), on-the-fly in Word by clicking on any toolbar with the right mouse button. This calls up a drop-down menu from which you can choose the toolbar you want displayed.

3 Call up this drop-down menu to quickly add or remove toolbars

4 Click a toolbar with the left mouse button to turn it on (or off)

Tip:

Click **Customize** on the menu to call up the Toolbars dialog box where you can change toolbars, commands and options

Toolbars (contd)

All default toolbars in Word are displayed below. While most appear initially fixed in position in the document window, you can move many of them by dragging them away from their initial positions — at which point they become floating toolbars, movable anywhere you might have some screen space suitable. Any new toolbars you create for yourself (page 147) float too.

As you work your way round Word 2000, you'll find that other toolbars appear too, dependent on what you are attempting to do. When you have finished that particular task, or switch to another, these toolbars will disappear again.

Finally, remember that you can customize default toolbars, as well as any of your own creations, by moving, removing, adding, or creating buttons (pages 146–7).

Buttons

Buttons on toolbars are graphically representative of their function. As a result it's easy to see what most of them do. However, some buttons are a little more obscure. Here the standard and formatting toolbar buttons are listed together with brief explanations.

Take note:

There are many more buttons hidden within Word's interface, either pre-formatted onto other toolbars, or unused in a default installation. There's nothing to stop you using or customizing these, or even creating your own buttons from scratch

- new document
- open document
- save document
- print document
- print preview
- spelling
- cut
- copy
- paste
- format painter
- undo
- redo
- insert hyperlink
- Web toolbar

- tables and borders
- insert address
- insert table
- insert Excel worksheet
- columns
- drawing
- document map
- show/hide ¶
- zoom control
- TipWizard
- Office Assistant
- style
- font
- font size

- bold
- italic
- underline
- align left
- align centre
- align right
- justify
- numbering
- bullets
- decrease indent
- increase indent
- borders
- highlight
- font colour

Normal view

Word allows a number of views of your document — normal view is simply the one new documents usually default to. It's important to remember, though, that each view of a document makes no difference to what's actually in the document — it's just one way of looking at it.

Basic steps:

1 Your document is probably already in normal view (see below). If not, choose **View � Normal**, or type `Alt`+`V` then `N`, or (best) click the Normal view button `≡` at the bottom left of your document window

1 Normal view

Put a coin in the slot to make me work. If you put two coins in, not only do I work, but I smile, sing and dance too.

Make my day now, I'll be back!

Normal view button

Web layout, print layout and outline view buttons

Web layout view

1 Choose **View⤷Web Layout**, or type `Alt`+`V` then `W`, or (best) click the Web layout view button at the bottom left of the document window

One of the hottest things in computing these days is hypertext markup language (HTML). Hypertext is the way some documents allow you to access related information merely by clicking a link (sometimes called a hyperlink, because of this). Pages displayed on the part of the Internet known as the World Wide Web are all created with hypertext markup language. Word 2000 allows you to create and view hypertext documents in Web layout view.

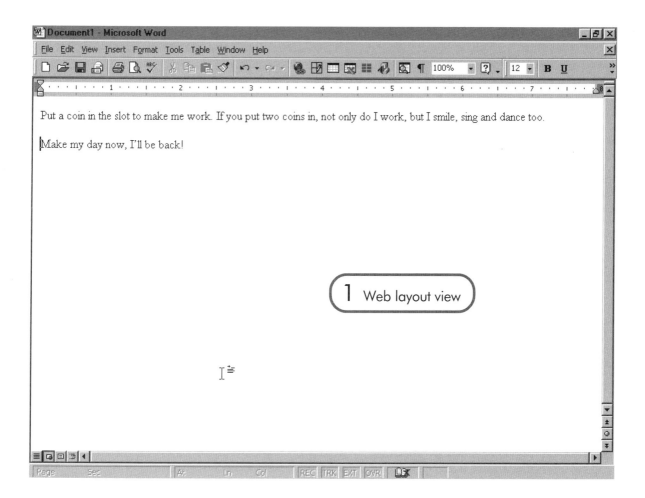

Put a coin in the slot to make me work. If you put two coins in, not only do I work, but I smile, sing and dance too.

Make my day now, I'll be back!

1 Web layout view

Print layout view

This view lets you see how the printed page will appear — *what you see is what you get* (WYSIWYG). Margins and borders around text are shown, as well as positions of graphics. This is a useful view to check the final appearance of your document before printing.

However, general operation becomes a little slower.

Basic steps:

1 Choose **View↬Print Layout**, or type `Alt`+`V` then `P`, or (best) click the Print layout button `≣` at the bottom left of your document window

1 Print layout view

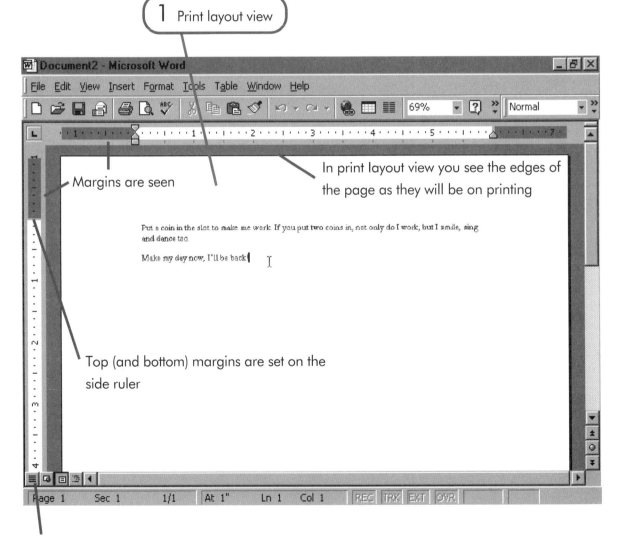

Margins are seen

In print layout view you see the edges of the page as they will be on printing

Put a coin in the slot to make me work. If you put two coins in, not only do I work, but I smile, sing and dance too.

Make my day now, I'll be back!

Top (and bottom) margins are set on the side ruler

Get back to normal view with this button

Outline view

1 Choose **View** ↳
   Outline, or type
   [Alt] + [V] then [O], or
   (best) click the Outline
   button [⊞] at the bottom
   left of your document
   window

Outline view allows you to control how the various levels of heading and subheadings in your document are displayed (or not displayed) and organised. It is the ideal method of rearranging documents by moving parts of text long distances within the document, or changing the hierarchy of headings. See page 102 for fuller details of outlining.

> 1   Outline view

```
W Document1 - Microsoft Word                                                    _ B X
File  Edit  View  Insert  Format  Tools  Table  Window  Help                         X
[toolbar icons]  100%  ▾  ?  ▾  12  ▾  B  U                                          »
← → ➡  ⬆ ⬇  ✦ –  1 2 3 4 5 6 7  All ═ ᴬ₄ □ ➡ □ □ □ □ □ □ .

        ▫  Put a coin in the slot to make me work. If you put two coins in, not only do I
           work, but I smile, sing and dance too.
        ▫
        ▫  Make my day now, I'll be back!
   —
```

The outline toolbar is automatically displayed in outline view – the numbers indicate which level of heading and subheading is applied

In outline view, text has bullets to show respective hierarchies of headings and subheadings. You can drag text around to suit, collapse text so that only headings are displayed, and rearrange heading level hierarchies

```
Page 1   Sec 1   1/1   At 1.5"   Ln 4   Col 1   REC TRK EXT OVR  □∃
```

Get back to normal view with this button

Full screen view

Word has a neat facility to get rid of all the on-screen clutter such as toolbars, menu line, and scroll boxes.

Basic steps:

1 Choose **View⤷Full Screen**, or type `Alt`+`V` then `U`

> Tip:
>
> **You can still access individual menus by moving the mouse pointer over the thick top edge of the window, or by typing `Alt`+the menu's underlined letter eg, `Alt`+`F` displays the File menu**

1 Full screen view

Put a coin in the slot to make me work. If you put two coins in, not only do I work, but I smile, sing and dance too.

Make my day now, I'll be back!

To get back to normal view, click the full screen button on the full screen toolbar

▾ Full Screen
Close Full Screen

Basic steps:

1 Click on the down arrow of the zoom control button of the standard toolbar

2 From the resultant drop-down menu, choose your desired zoom percentage

3 As an alternative you can choose **View**↳**Zoom**, to call up the **Zoom** dialog box, and select a zoom value there

You can magnify or reduce part of a document page in Word, to get a close up or overall view of the page. This is known as zooming.

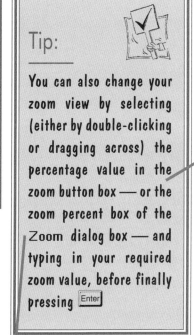

Tip:

You can also change your zoom view by selecting (either by double-clicking or dragging across) the percentage value in the zoom button box — or the zoom percent box of the Zoom dialog box — and typing in your required zoom value, before finally pressing Enter

1 Drop-down menu appears as you click the zoom button down arrow

2 Choose your required zoom percentage from the menu list

3 The **Zoom** dialog box

Choose your zoom percentage here

A preview gives you some idea of text size

Saving a document

Once you've worked on a document you need to save it onto disk:

● the document remains in computer memory only as long as Word is running

● if you quit Word, or turn off your machine without saving the document to disk it is lost forever — **RIP**

1 Choose **File→Save**, or type [Alt]+[F] then [S], or type [Ctrl]+[S], or click the Save button [🖫]. The first time you do this, the **Save As** dialog box is called up

2 Enter a name in the **File Name** box

3 Locate the folder you want, then click **Save** to save the document

1 The **Save As** dialog box

3 Locate the folder to save in, then click **Save**

2 Enter a document name here, or use the suggested default (which is the first line of your document)

Opening documents

1 Choose **File→Open**, or type `Alt`+`F` then `O`, or type `Ctrl`+`O`, or click the Open button ⌂. The **Open** dialog box is shown

2 Locate the document you wish to open in its drive and folder

3 Click **Open**

When you first start up Word a new document is created automatically for you, ready for you to enter text. Usually, this new document is of a standard form.

There are times, however, when you may need to open another style of document to use as your new one, or even just open existing documents you have previously saved. If you have worked on these documents recently, you might find them listed in the **Documents** folder of the 🔖Start menu, but if it's been a while since using them, you can open them from within Word.

1 **Open** dialog box

2 Find the document to open

3 Click here

If the document isn't a Word document, this drop-down box lets you see other openable document types

Creating new documents

Creating a new document is just as easy as opening an existing document. Word creates a new document as the image of a template. Templates are ready-built and installed document *plans*, complete with styles and formats you might want to use for any particular appearance of document (see page 134 for further details of templates).

Templates are arranged in sections, accessed in the **New Office Document** dialog box with tabs.

1 **New Office Document** dialog box

2 Click a tab

3 Select a template

4 Click **OK**

Basing on existing documents

BASED ON EXISTING DOCUMENTS

1 On the desktop, locate the folder holding the Word document you want to create a new copy from

2 Click the document with the right mouse button

3 In the shortcut menu, click **New** with your left mouse button – a copy of the document is opened

You can create new documents from other documents, too. If you have, say, a letter (or in this example, a fax) that you have previously written, and decide that it is in the same format as another you want to send, you can simply open it and change the details you need to change, saving considerable time.

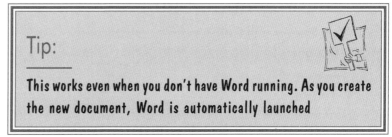

Tip:

This works even when you don't have Word running. As you create the new document, Word is automatically launched

1 Locate the document

3 With your left mouse button, click **New**

2 Click the document with the right mouse button

Goodbye – or au revoir ?

Basic steps:

After you've finished using a computer program it's usual to exit or quit it. If you're only trying to clear the screen for a short while, on the other hand, there are alternatives.

1 **Save Changes** dialog box when the Office Assistant is not running

Microsoft Word

Do you want to save the changes you made to "Put a coin in the slot to make me work"?

Yes | No | Cancel

2 Click to save. If you have not saved the document before this, the **Save As** dialog box will be displayed (see page 18)

Tip:

You don't actually have to quit programs before you shut down your computer. Just choose Start **→Shut Down, and the computer exits all your open programs correctly, presenting the required Save Changes dialog boxes to suit**

QUITTING OR EXITING WORD

1 Choose **File→Exit**, or type Alt + F then X. If you have recently saved the document or documents you are working on and have not worked on them since, Word quits straightaway. If you have worked on a document since last saving it (or have not saved it at all) the **Save Changes?** dialog box is displayed. This varies depending on whether you have the Office Assistant running or not

2 If you have not saved a document recently, click **Yes**

Microsoft Word

Do you want to save the changes you made to "Put a coin in the slot to make me work"?

Yes | No | Cancel

1 **Save Changes** dialog box when the Office Assistant is running

1 Click Word's **Minimize** button , at the top right corner

2 Click the window's button created on the Taskbar, to restore the window to its previous size and position

Temporarily clearing your screen

If you're only trying to clear your screen for a short while — and you don't want to quit Word — click the **Minimize** button ⬛ at the top right of the Word program window. This minimizes the program window as a button, left on the taskbar — showing the document name (as long as it's not too long) — as well as its creator (Microsoft Word).

Take note:

While the technique here works for a Word 2000 program window, it doesn't work for individual document windows. Previous versions of Word allowed you to minimize individual document windows within the program window as well as the complete program window, but Word 2000 only allows you minimize the complete program window

While minimizing can be confusing for a new user, used properly it can help clear up your desktop. However, it's best to remember that programs should not be left long term in this mode — exiting them correctly clears up computer memory for other tasks

1 Click the **Minimize** button here

2 The window, along with any other minimized windows are displayed along the Taskbar. Click a button to restore a window

23

Summary

❑ Start up Word by choosing **[⚑Start]**↳**Programs**↳
Microsoft Word, or **[⚑Start]**↳**Programs**↳**Microsoft
Office**↳**Microsoft Word** from the taskbar.

❑ Get on-line help by clicking the Office Assistant button **[?]**
in the standard toolbar.

❑ Access toolbars by either clicking on any toolbar with the
right mouse button then selecting the one you want, or
choose **View**↳**Toolbars** to call up the **Toolbars** dialog
box.

❑ Change document view between normal, Web layout, print
layout, outline and full-screen views to suit the way you
work.

❑ Print layout view lets you see the page as it will be printed.

❑ Outline view lets you rearrange headings and their hierarchies, as well as dragging text large distances easily in the
document.

❑ Remove all on-screen clutter with full screen view by
choosing **View**↳**Full Screen**

❑ Open existing Word documents – or other applications'
documents – from the **Open** dialog box.

❑ Create a new document – in the form of a selected
template – in the **New** dialog box.

24

2   Text essentials

Entering text

As a word processor, of course, Word's main function is to store straightforward text. As you start up Word, or create a new document, you can begin to enter text immediately.

Basic steps:

1 Simply type something. It doesn't matter what – a few lines of rubbish will do nicely

2 If your document is important, remember to save it

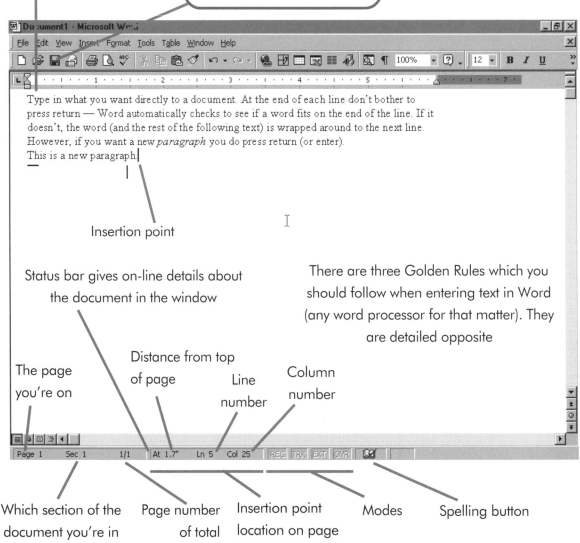

1 Enter text into document

2 Click the save button 🖫 to save your document

Type in what you want directly to a document. At the end of each line don't bother to press return — Word automatically checks to see if a word fits on the end of the line. If it doesn't, the word (and the rest of the following text) is wrapped around to the next line. However, if you want a new *paragraph* you do press return (or enter).
This is a new paragraph.

Insertion point

Status bar gives on-line details about the document in the window

There are three Golden Rules which you should follow when entering text in Word (any word processor for that matter). They are detailed opposite

Distance from top of page

Column number

Line number

The page you're on

Which section of the document you're in

Page number of total

Insertion point location on page

Modes

Spelling button

26

The status bar

Get into the habit of looking at the status bar. It gives some explicit information about what's happening within your Word document, such as:

❑ page number, section (you can break your document up into smaller sections, to make it more manageable – see page 72) number, and total number of pages

❑ location of the insertion point (that is, the point within text where your keyboard entries appear on screen)

❑ mode buttons – accessed by double-clicking – of these only two are of importance here, and are:

❑ WPH – on-line help for ex-WordPerfect users

❑ OVR – active when blacked (that is, not greyed). See next page for details

❑ spelling button – if the button displays an ✗ mark, Word has detected a spelling error

Take note:

The Golden Rules of Word

1 Never, never, never, never, never, never, never, never, never, never (get the message?) put two spaces together. The old typists' routine of putting two spaces at the end of a sentence should not be done in a word processor because spaces aren't generally of a fixed width. A program like Word adjusts spaces to ensure the text fits its given column width and looks good. Two or more spaces together may be adjusted in width to give ridiculously wide spaces between words. For the same reason, text which is formed into tabular columns mustn't be created by inserting spaces to line columns up — it might look aligned on screen, but when it prints you can't guarantee it — use proper tabs instead (see page 58)

2 Never, never, never, never (oh, here we go again) put two carriage returns together. Actually, this isn't quite so critical as Golden Rule number 1, but important nevertheless. Spaces between paragraphs are best controlled by creating styles for each paragraph type (see Chapter 6) which incorporate spaces before and after them

3 Never (once is enough this time, I'm sure) press ⏎ or Enter at the end of a line of text — unless the end of the line is also the end of a paragraph. There is simply no need — and carriage returns fix the text to those line lengths. Use Word's word-wrapping facility to do it automatically — then any textual style changes will automatically create consequent new word-wraps

Editing text

Inevitably you will make mistakes in your work. This is where a word processor like Word shows its strength — mistakes can be simply edited on-screen before printing. Even if a mistake slips by you, and you only see it after printing, you can correct it and reprint the document.

Even if your required corrections aren't due to mistakes, but are straightforward editorial changes, Word has some unbeaten facilities for making any kind of textual change necessary in a document.

There are several ways you can edit text. The simplest — covered here — is *overtyping*.

All editing procedures, on the other hand, rely on the principle of placing the insertion point at the point which requires editing! If you learn nothing else from this page, learn this fact.

OVERTYPE EDITING

1 If you spot a mistake which requires you to retype part or all of a word or sentence, position the insertion point at the beginning of the mistake

2 Look at the `OVR` button on the status bar. If it is greyed, you are in insert edit mode, if it is black you are in overtype edit mode. Double-click it to toggle between the two modes. Make sure you are in overtype edit mode (the button should be in blackface (ie `OVR`)

1 As you move the mouse pointer over text it changes to the I-beam pointer ⌶. When you position the pointer over the point to edit then click, the insertion point of Word becomes active at that point. This whole process of pointing and clicking with the I-beam pointer ⌶ is known as positioning the insertion point.

Remember it – because all editing relies on it!

There was a cow stupefied on a hill. If it hasn't gonn it will be their still.
Now is the time for all good men to come to the aid of the party

3 Retype the section of text – this overtypes text already there

4 Move to any other areas you need to overtype as in Step 1

5 When you have finished overtyping double-click the overtype button `OVR` again, to return to insertion mode

Take note:

Editing in any word processor worth its salt is most often a combination of techniques — not just one. In other words: find out about all techniques — these shown here, as well as those shown over following pages — to take full advantage of Word. Word is an immensely powerful computer program. If you don't take advantage of its power you're not using your computer efficiently

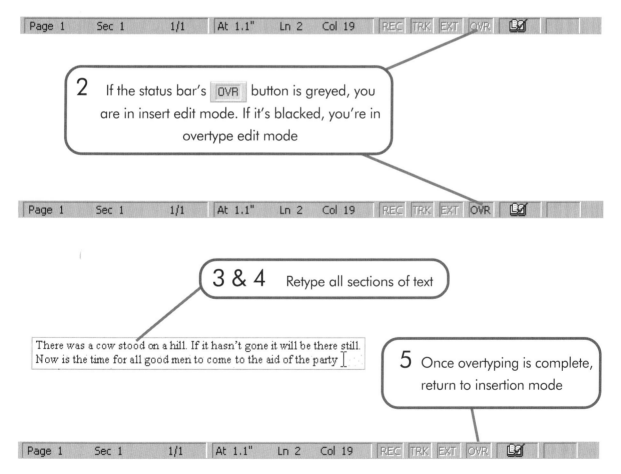

| Page 1 | Sec 1 | 1/1 | At 1.1" | Ln 2 | Col 19 | REC | TRK | EXT | OVR | |

2 If the status bar's `OVR` button is greyed, you are in insert edit mode. If it's blacked, you're in overtype edit mode

| Page 1 | Sec 1 | 1/1 | At 1.1" | Ln 2 | Col 19 | REC | TRK | EXT | OVR | |

3 & 4 Retype all sections of text

There was a cow stood on a hill. If it hasn't gone it will be there still. Now is the time for all good men to come to the aid of the party

5 Once overtyping is complete, return to insertion mode

| Page 1 | Sec 1 | 1/1 | At 1.1" | Ln 2 | Col 19 | REC | TRK | EXT | OVR | |

Selecting text

Basic steps:

Whenever you want to edit text (that is, apart from when you overtype — see previous page) you need to select the particular text you want to change:

● Word allows you to do this in various ways

● no single way is best

● instead, a combination of selecting techniques — depending on what is to be selected — should be used

● selection of text is sometimes known by different names such as blocking or highlighting. These names are often merely descriptive of the selection process — text which is selected becomes highlighted or blocked and that's how you know the text happens to be selected!

1 You can select any letter, word, sentence, paragraph, or any part of these by dragging over the required text

2 To select a single word, double-click the word

3 To select more than one word, drag from one word across to the next, or further if you want more words to be selected

4 To select a whole line of text, click in the selection bar to the left of the line

contd…

1 Drag the I-beam pointer I over the letters, or words, or sentences, or paragraphs you want to be selected

No, no, no, said the Giant. There can be no suggestion of a compromise. I am going to eat you all up, because that's the sort of thing giants are known to do.

2 You can select a single word most quickly by double-clicking the word

No, no, no, said the Giant. There can be no suggsetion of a compromise. I am going to eat you all up, because that's the sort of thing giants are known to do.

As you drag over your selected text and release the mouse button, the selected text becomes highlighted.

Highlighted text is simply the visible sign that the text is selected

30

3 Drag over words to select them. As you drag over each new part of a word the whole word becomes selected automatically

No, no, no, said the Giant. There can be no suggsetion of a compromise. I am going to eat you all up, because that's the sort of thing giants are known to do.

Tip:

When you begin selecting in the middle of a word, then drag to include part of another word, Word automatically selects both words (and any subsequent ones too), as well as any space after the words

4 Select whole lines of text by clicking in the selection bar

No, no, no, said the Giant. There can be no suggsetion of a compromise. I am going to eat you all up, because that's the sort of thing giants are known to do.

The selection bar is to the left of text on any Word document page

Take note:

All of these selection techniques can be used to select graphic items, such as pictures, as well as text

Selecting text (contd)

No, no, no, said the Giant. There can be no suggsetion of a compromise. I am going to eat you all up, because that's the sort of thing giants are known to do.

5 Select multiple lines of text by dragging in the selection bar

No, no, no, said the Giant. There can be no suggsetion of a compromise. I am going to eat you all up, because that's the sort of thing giants are known to do.

6 Select a single sentence by holding down `Ctrl` and clicking in the sentence

No, no, no, said the Giant. There can be no suggsetion of a compromise. I am going to eat you all up, because that's the sort of thing giants are known to do.

7 Double-click in the selection bar (or triple-click in the text) to select a paragraph

No, no, no, said the Giant. There can be no suggsetion of a compromise. I am going to eat you all up, because that's the sort of thing giants are known to do.

8 Drag across paragraphs in the selection bar to select multiple paragraphs

No, no, no, said the Giant. There can be no suggsetion of a compromise. I am going to eat you all up, because that's the sort of thing giants are known to do.

With that he picked up Jack and lifted him towards his mouth. Once inside the Giant's mouth Jack realised his time was nigh unless he did some quick thinking. He decided to go for broke and tickled the Giant's tonsils.

5 To select multiple lines of text, drag in the selection bar to the left of the lines

6 To select a sentence, hold down `Ctrl` and click anywhere in the sentence

7 To select a paragraph, either double-click in the selection bar to the left of the paragraph, or triple-click anywhere in the text

8 To select multiple paragraphs, drag in the selection bar to the left of the paragraphs

9 To select an entire document, triple-click in the selection bar

10 Select text which is neither a whole word, sentence, or paragraph by positioning the insertion point at the beginning of the text, then holding down `Shift` while you click at the text end

9 Select an entire document's text by triple-clicking in the selection bar

> Take two aspirins and call me in the mroning. The dogs sat on the mat. When the Queen of Hearts had no tea the Knave of Hearts stole the tarts. Instead she beat the Knave of Hearts soundly and sent him to bed.
>
> No, no, no, said the Giant. There can be no suggsetion of a compromise. I am going to eat you all up, because that's the sort of thing giants are known to do.
>
> With that he picked up Jack and lifted him towards his mouth. Once inside the Giant's mouth Jack realised his time was nigh unless he did some quick thinking. He decided to go for broke and tickled the Giant's tonsils.

Tip:

Cancel a selection by clicking outside it, or pressing any arrow key

10 By clicking at the starting point, then holding down [Shift] and clicking at the finishing point, a complete block of text can be selected

> No, no, no, said the Giant. There can be no suggsetion of a compromise. I am going to eat you all up, because that's the sort of thing giants are known to do.
>
> With that he picked up Jack and lifted him towards his mouth. Once inside the Giant's mouth Jack realised his time was nigh unless he did some quick thinking. He decided to go for broke and tickled the Giant's tonsils.

KEYBOARD SHORTCUTS

You can select text with the keyboard too:

One character right	[Shift] + [→]
One character left	[Shift] + [←]
To the end of a word	[Ctrl] + [Shift] + [→]
To the beginning of a word	[Ctrl] + [Shift] + [←]
To the end of a line	[Shift] + [End]
To the beginning of a line	[Shift] + [Home]
One line down	[Shift] + [↓]
One line up	[Shift] + [↑]
To the end of a paragraph	[Ctrl] + [Shift] + [↓]
To the start of a paragraph	[Ctrl] + [Shift] + [↑]
One screen down	[Shift] + [Page Down]
One screen up	[Shift] + [Page Up]
To end of document	[Ctrl] + [Shift] + [End]
To beginning of document	[Ctrl] + [Shift] + [Home]
Entire document	[Ctrl] + [A]
To a specific location	[F8] +arrow keys

Tip:

Whatever you do in Word — writing, editing, stylising, formatting and so on — relies on you being able to select text.

No single selection method is best for all purposes. Depending on what you want to select, you should choose the preferred method. Sometimes you should use the mouse, sometimes you should use the keyboard.

The only way you can make sure you use the preferred method for any particular purpose is to learn how to use all methods

Ooops – a mistake!

Word processors are meant to make the correction of mistakes as simple as possible. Apart from the proper editing facilities of Word we've already seen, however, are extra goodies which make the correction of simple typing errors almost as easy as making the mistakes in the first place — but not qwite, if you see what I mean!

It's as well to know all these goodies to get the best out of Word. The mistakes we're concerned with here are those which you notice almost as you make them:

● obvious spelling errors

● mis-hit keys

● style changes which shouldn't have been made

and so on.

1 If you have just a few letters you want to delete, a quick result can be to press ⌫, or delete:

❏ ⌫ deletes the character before the insertion point

❏ delete deletes the character after the insertion point

❏ Ctrl + ⌫ deletes the word before the insertion point

❏ Ctrl + delete deletes the word after the insertion point

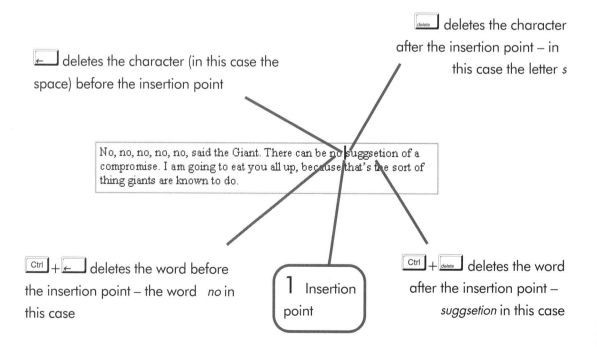

⌫ deletes the character (in this case the space) before the insertion point

delete deletes the character after the insertion point – in this case the letter *s*

> No, no, no, no, no, said the Giant. There can be no suggsetion of a compromise. I am going to eat you all up, because that's the sort of thing giants are known to do.

Ctrl + ⌫ deletes the word before the insertion point – the word *no* in this case

1 Insertion point

Ctrl + delete deletes the word after the insertion point – *suggsetion* in this case

2 You can very often undo a mistake or change you make in a Word document, because Word features a multiple undo facility. Just click the Undo button 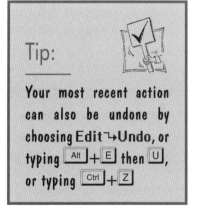 after you have made a mistake or change you want to undo and a drop-down box lists all your recent actions in reverse order – your most recent action at the top of the list

Tip:

Your most recent action can also be undone by choosing Edit→Undo, or typing [Alt]+[E] then [U], or typing [Ctrl]+[Z]

Tip:

If you undo an action by mistake, click the Redo button to undo the undo!

Take note:

Actions can only be undone in strict order — if you want to undo the action 48 places down the list, the most recent 47 actions have to be undone also!

2 Clicking the Undo button displays a drop-down list box

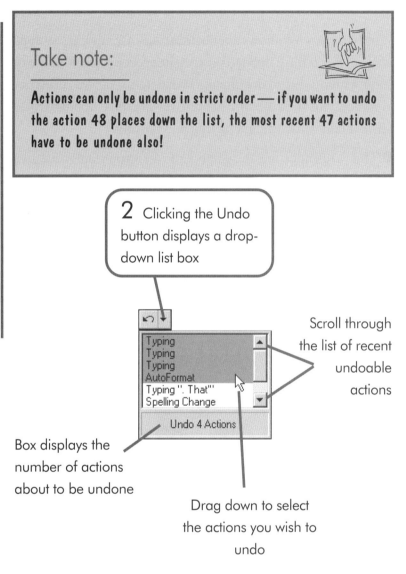

Scroll through the list of recent undoable actions

Box displays the number of actions about to be undone

Drag down to select the actions you wish to undo

Take note:

While Word's undo feature is a boon for those of us who make mistakes — that is, anyone who uses a computer — you should remember that some actions are not undoable

Cut, copy and paste

Word (like any Windows application) uses a temporary storage area known as the Clipboard to keep items you want to move or copy within a Word document. These items can be of text or graphic forms (or a mixture of both). Using the Clipboard to do this is known as cutting, copying and pasting:

● you *cut* an item onto the Clipboard when you want to remove it from one place in a document and move it to another place

● you *copy* an item onto the Clipboard when you want it to occur at more than one place in your document

● taking an item from the Clipboard and putting it in your document is known as *pasting*.

CUTTING

1 Select the item or items you want to cut onto the Clipboard. This can be a selection of text, a graphical item, or a combination of the two

2 Choose **Edit**↪**Cut**, or type [Alt]+[E] then [T], or type [Ctrl]+[X], or simply click the Cut button [✄] to cut the selected item – it disappears from your Word document and is moved onto the Clipboard

---

Come and see the show

On the other hand, this is a boring part of this document. Let's liven it up by moving the graphic down here!

1 & 3 Select the item or items to be cut or copied

Use whichever selection method is appropriate for the text (or graphic in this case) to be copied or cut. To select this graphic, clicking in the selection bar is fastest

2 Cut the item or items (now you see it – now you don't!)

Come and see the show

On the other hand, this is a boring part of this document. Let's liven it up by moving the graphic down here!

5 Position the insertion point before pasting

I

3 Select the item or items you want to copy

4 Choose **Edit→Copy**, or type `Alt`+`E` then `C`, or type `Ctrl`+`C`, or click the Copy button 📋 – the selection stays in your document but is copied onto the Clipboard too

5 Position the insertion point where you want the item or items stored on the Clipboard to be pasted

6 Choose **Edit→Paste**, or type `Alt`+`E` then `P`, or type `Ctrl`+`V`, or click the Paste button 📋 to paste the item or items into your document

Tip:

Word has a Clipboard that can hold up to 12 items. The Clipboard is shared with other Office 2000 programs, so items can be copied from one program and pasted into another

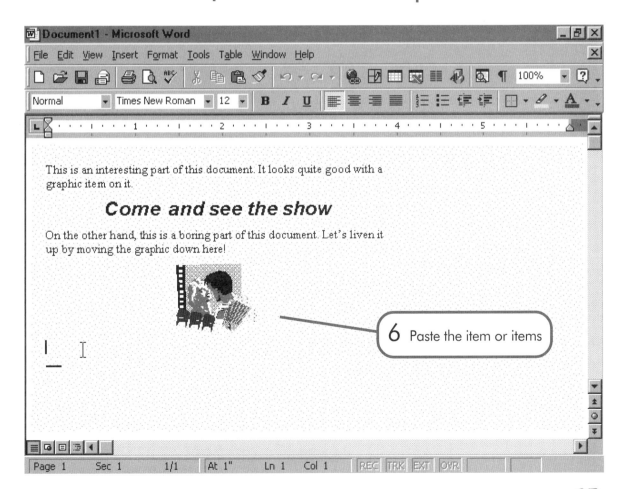

6 Paste the item or items

Drag-and-drop editing

Word has an extremely useful feature in its ability to allow selected text to be moved or copied by dragging. Proper use of drag-and-drop editing can speed up incorporation of revisions in a document.

> 1 Select the text

Take two aspirins and call me in the mroning. The dogs sat on the mat. When the Queen of Hearts had no tea the Knave of Hearts stole the tarts. Instead she beat the Knave of Hearts soundly and sent him to bed.

> 2 The arrow pointer replaces the I-beam pointer over selected text

Take two aspirins and call me in the mroning. The dogs sat on the mat. When the Queen of Hearts had no tea the Knave of Hearts stole the tarts. Instead she beat the Knave of Hearts soundly and sent him to bed.

> 3 As you drag the selected text, the drag-and-drop pointer is displayed

Take two aspirins and call me in the mroning. The dogs sat on the mat. When the Queen of Hearts had no tea the Knave of Hearts stole the tarts. Instead she beat the Knave of Hearts soundly and sent him to bed.

> 4 The dotted insertion point tells you where the text will be moved to

> 5 The text moves as you let go the mouse button

Take two aspirins and call me in the mroning. The dogs sat on the mat. When the Knave of Hearts stole the tarts the Queen of Hearts had no tea. Instead she beat the Knave of Hearts soundly and sent him to bed.

MOVING SELECTED TEXT

1 Select the text to be moved

2 Position the pointer over the selected text (the I-beam pointer ⌶ changes to the arrow pointer ⌖)

3 Click on the selected text and drag the pointer – it changes to the drag-and-drop pointer

4 As you drag the drag-and-drop pointer to a new position, the dotted insertion point follows indicating where the selected text will be dragged to

5 When you have located the dotted insertion point where you want, release the mouse button. The selected text moves to the new location

38

COPYING SELECTED TEXT

6 Select text as before

7 Drag the selected text as before

8 Locate the position you wish to copy text to as before (with the dotted insertion point)

9 Before you let go the mouse button, press and hold down `Ctrl` (the drag-and-drop pointer changes to show a plus symbol indicating Word is ready to copy – that is, not just move – text)

10 Let go the mouse button. The selected text is copied to the new location

---

Tip:

Drag-and-drop editing is really just an extension of the cut, copy and paste principle. As a result, you can drag-and-drop graphical items, or a combination of graphical *and* text items, as well as just text

---

No, no, no, said the Giant. There can be no suggsetion of a compromise. I am going to eat you all up, because that's the sort of thing giants are known to do.

6 Select text to be copied

7 Drag selected text with drag-and-drop pointer

No, no, no, said the Giant. There can be no suggsetion of a compromise. I am going to eat you all up, because that's the sort of thing giants are known to do.

8 Locate the dotted insertion point where you want the text to be copied to

No, no, no, said the Giant. There can be no suggsetion of a compromise. I am going to eat you all up, because that's the sort of thing giants are known to do.

9 Hold down `Ctrl` to copy selected text (indicated by + symbol on drag-and-drop pointer)

10 As you release the mouse button, selected text is copied

No, no, no, no, no, said the Giant. There can be no suggsetion of a compromise. I am going to eat you all up, because that's the sort of thing giants are known to do.

Entering symbols

Although Word is a *word* processor, very often it's necessary to include symbols within text. Examples of such symbols are:

● mathematical or scientific symbols — Ω μ ß ∝ for example (however, if you want to include more than just a couple of mathematical formulae or expressions into your work it is best to use Word's integral equation editor, which is beyond the scope of this book)

● dingbats — the blob or bullet (●) at the left of this list is an example of a dingbat. Others are ✂ ☞ ♣ ❑ ♠ which can be used to embellish text

● typographical symbols and marks — the most obvious examples of typographical marks are the so-called curly quotes (' and ") which differentiate properly typeset text as you would find in a book from ordinary word processed (with straight quotes — ' and ") text, together with other typeset additions such as en dashes (–) and em dashes (—)

● foreign letters with accents — é ü å õ ç

and so on.

The ability to enter such symbols rapidly greatly enhances a word processor. Word has a special Symbol command which simplifies the task.

Basic steps:

1 Position the insertion point where you want the symbol to be (if you are typing in text and want to enter the symbol as you go, the insertion point is already positioned correctly). Now choose **Insert→Symbol**, or type `Alt`+`I` then `S`. This calls up the **Symbol** dialog box which automatically displays symbols available in fonts

2 Click a symbol and it is displayed enlarged. Click Insert if you want the symbol in your text. Alternatively, double-click the symbol you want. It is placed in text at the position of the insertion point

3 Display and choose a different font if you want with the **Font** drop-down list box

Tip:

Use typographer's symbols and marks to give your work that professional edge. Automatically include curly quotes using Word's AutoCorrect feature (page 98). Use an en dash to combine number ranges (eg, pages 40–41) and use an em dash to separate emphasising text — just like that!

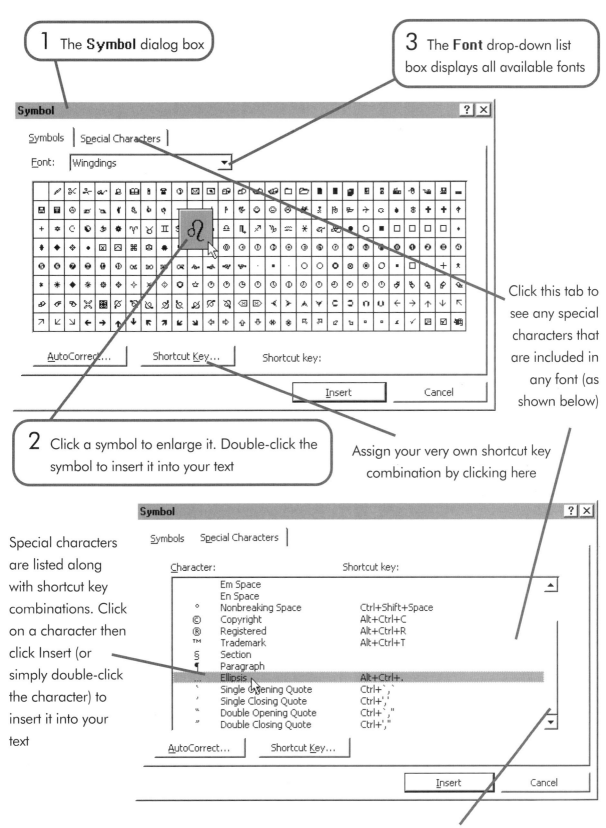

1 The **Symbol** dialog box

3 The **Font** drop-down list box displays all available fonts

Click this tab to see any special characters that are included in any font (as shown below)

2 Click a symbol to enlarge it. Double-click the symbol to insert it into your text

Assign your very own shortcut key combination by clicking here

Special characters are listed along with shortcut key combinations. Click on a character then click Insert (or simply double-click the character) to insert it into your text

Scroll through the list to see more characters

41

Summary

❑ Follow the three Golden Rules of Word:

   1 never put two spaces together

   2 never put two carriage returns together

   3 never press ⏎ or Enter at the end of a line of text – unless it is also the end of a paragraph.

❑ Get into the habit of checking the status bar regularly.

❑ Learn how to select text using all of the available methods – no one method is best for all cases, and you really need to know them all.

❑ Word's multiple undo feature can save you hours of work if you make a mistake.

❑ Use the cut, copy and paste facility to speed up your work. Learn the keyboard shortcuts (Ctrl + X to cut, Ctrl + C to copy, Ctrl + V to paste), or use the toolbar buttons (✂ , 📋 , and 📋).

❑ Use drag-and-drop editing – although a little tricky to get the hang of, it's an extremely good editing aid.

❑ Access symbols and special characters with the **Symbol** dialog box.

❑ Use typographer's special marks and symbols to give your work a truly professional look.

3 Formatting text

About formatting

When you first enter text at the keyboard in Word it is generally unformatted. That is, it is plain, unembellished, with no changes applied to alter its appearance. Generally, it will be in the default font (say, Times New Roman) and a default size (say, 10 point).

Making alterations to text's appearance is known as formatting the text. There are several ways this can be done in Word:

● formatting can be applied by the user to individual or grouped characters — this is known as *character formatting*

● formatting can be applied by the user to whole paragraphs — called (fancy that) *paragraph formatting*

● formatting can be applied automatically by Word — either as you enter text or afterwards, and either across a whole document (using Word's *AutoFormat* feature), or to paragraphs (using *paragraph styles*).

While character and paragraph formatting are both very powerful tools and can give you the visual effects you might require in a document, the *real* power of a word processor like Word lies in its ability to apply automatic formatting.

Take note:

Use character and paragraph formatting by all means — and they're going to be described over the next few pages so you can get to grips with them — but bear in mind that only when you use them to build *automatic* formatting features do they *really* become useful

You can format whole lines

You can format individual characters or words

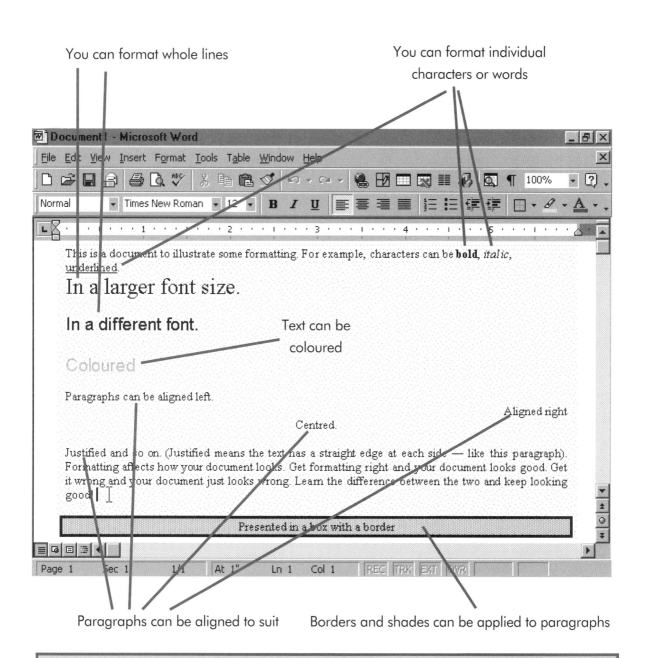

Text can be coloured

Paragraphs can be aligned to suit

Borders and shades can be applied to paragraphs

Character formats

Character formatting is a matter of selecting the text you wish to format, then applying the format change you want.

Many of the most common formats are available as buttons or options on the formatting toolbar. Some, however, are accessed by menu choice.

1 Select the text to be formatted

2 Apply the new format or formats

---

1 Select the text to be formatted – this can be an individual letter, a word, group of words, sentence, paragraph, or even the whole document

This is a sample of text in Times New Roman font at 10 point. It will be used to **illustrate character formatting**.

2 Format the selected text to suit – this example shows the selected text emboldened

This is a sample of text in Times New Roman font at 10 point. It will be used to **illustrate character formatting**.

Tip:

To format a single word you don't need to select the word in the usual manner — all you have to do is click anywhere in the word, then apply the format changes you want

Text you format is displayed formatted on screen. There are no formatting codes (as in some – let's say – lesser-capable word processors). What-you-see on-screen is more-or-less what-you-get on printout

Basic steps:

1 The formatting toolbar gives the easiest options to change common formats

There are three main ways you can apply formatting:

1 From the formatting toolbar – buttons or options

Click buttons to apply (or remove) bold, italic, and underline

Change font with this drop-down list box – if you have many fonts in your system you can jump in the list by entering the font's initial letter in the font name box – the list jumps directly to fonts with that initial letter for you to select

Change font size with this drop-down list box

If the font size you want isn't listed, just enter your desired size at the keyboard – if you are using a TrueType or PostScript font (shown by an icon in the font drop-down box – see left) it will display and print correctly for just about any size you want

The fonts you've used most recently are listed in the top of the list, above this line

A TrueType font

A font available on the printer currently selected

All fonts are listed alphabetically below the line

If your formatting toolbar is coupled with your standard toolbar (sometimes Word is installed like this), the whole of the toolbar is not displayed. Click the button at the end of the toolbar to display the missing toolbar items, then click the drop-down boxes as shown above

47

Character formats (contd)

From the **Font** dialog box
(choose **Format↳Font**,
or type `Alt`+`O` then `F`
to display it)

The **Font** dialog box gives
some more formatting
options

Click this tab to see more
options regarding letter
spacing and vertical
positioning

List box for font size

List box for
available fonts

Drop-down list
box for special
underlining
effects

List box of font
style format
options

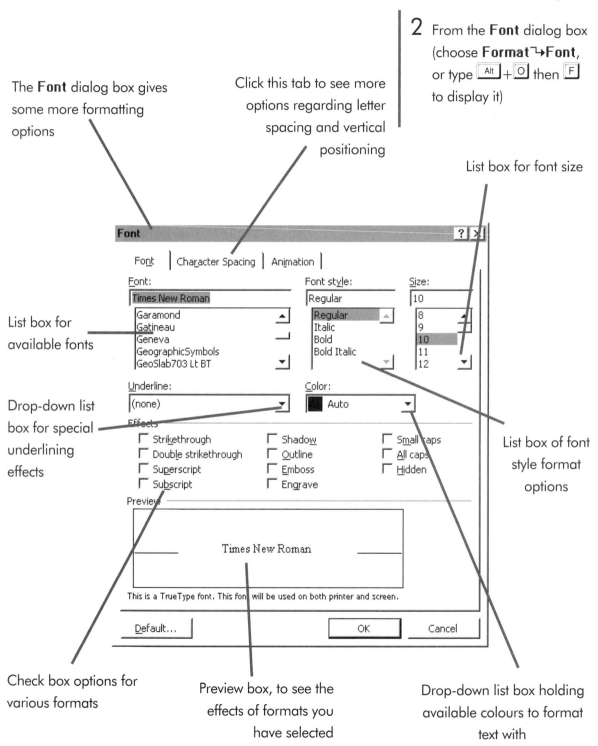

Check box options for
various formats

Preview box, to see the
effects of formats you
have selected

Drop-down list box holding
available colours to format
text with

3 With keyboard combinations. These can very often provide the quickest methods of applying formats

Many formatting options can best be applied with a keyboard shortcut:

Bold .... `Ctrl` + `B`

Italic .... `Ctrl` + `I`

Underline... `Ctrl` + `U`

Word underline .... `Ctrl` + `Shift` + `W`

Double underline .... `Ctrl` + `Shift` + `D`

Subscript .... `Ctrl` + `=`

Superscript .... `Ctrl` + `Shift` + `=`

Change selected text to small caps .... `Ctrl` + `Shift` + `K`

Change selected text to all caps .... `Ctrl` + `Shift` + `A`

Change case .... `Shift` + `F3`

Copy formats .... `Ctrl` + `Shift` + `C`

Paste formats .... `Ctrl` + `Shift` + `V`

Remove formats .... `Ctrl` +spacebar

Font .... `Ctrl` + `Shift` + `F`

Change to symbol font .... `Ctrl` + `Shift` + `Q`

Point size .... `Ctrl` + `Shift` + `P`, then enter font size you want

next up .... `Ctrl` + `>`

next down .... `Ctrl` + `<`

up one point .... `Ctrl` + `]`

down one point .... `Ctrl` + `[`

Tip:
___

You can apply a format to the insertion point too. This way, anything you type after the format is applied has that format, until you change it again. This is useful for, say, italicising a single word for emphasis as you type it — just apply the italic format (say, type `Ctrl` + `I`) before you type the word, then remove the italic format (type `Ctrl` + `I` again) hence returning to regular text after the word is finished

Character formats (contd)

There's a few points worth remembering about character formatting in Word. These are shown here as tips for you to use as reference.

Tip:

Your last formatting action can be repeated by choosing Edit↪Repeat Formatting, or typing Alt + E then R, or typing Ctrl + Y.

Note that all formats applied via the Font dialog box will be reapplied as one, whereas only the last individual formatting action applied with, say, buttons on the Formatting toolbar is reapplied

Tip:

Removing a character format follows the same procedure as applying it in the first place. You first select the character, characters, word, words, sentence, paragraph and so on, then you go through the same steps you took to originally apply it. If a word is emboldened, for example, simply select it then click the Bold button **B** on the formatting toolbar to remove the format

Tip:

You can remove *all* formatting applied by the methods shown over these last few pages to text, by first selecting the text then typing

Ctrl +spacebar

Note, though, that this does not remove formatting applied as part of styles (see page 120)

Painting a format

1 Select the text, part of text, or simply position the insertion point anywhere inside the text you wish to copy the formatting from

2 Click the Format Painter button ✎ on the Standard toolbar. The pointer changes to the format painter pointer ⏁

3 Select the text you want to be formatted with that format

If you see text which is formatted the way you want another selection of text to be formatted, you can copy the formatting onto further text with the Format Painter button ✎ on the Standard toolbar.

1 Select the text with the format you want to copy (in this case an italicised word)

Take it from me. There's no *point* in trying to pass your driving test. Within ten years at most — more likely five — there'll be so many cars on the road that no-one will be able to drive more than 35 miles per hour anyway. And where's the fun in that?

2 Click ✎   3 Select the text to be formatted

Take it from me. There's no *point* in trying to pass your driving test. Within ten years at most — more likely five — there'll be so many cars on the road that no-one will be able to drive more than 35 miles ⏁ hour anyway. And where's the fun in that?

Once selected, the text is automatically formatted

Take it from me. There's no *point* in trying to pass your driving test. Within ten years at most — more likely five — there'll be so many cars on the road that no-one will be able to *drive more than 35 miles per* hour anyway. And where's the fun in that?   I

Tip:

If you double-click the Format Painter button ✎ after selecting text with the format you want to copy, the format painter pointer ⏁ remains active after you have painted the format to further text. Continue to paint the format for as long as you want onto more selections of text. Click the Format Painter button again to de-activate

Tip:

You don't even need to select a single word if you want to paint another word's format onto it with the format painter pointer ⏁. Just click anywhere inside the word and the format is painted over the whole word

Paragraph formats

Whereas character formats affect just the *characters* you select, paragraph formats control the — you've got it — *paragraphs*. In other words, complete blocks of text and their line spacings, indents or alignments for example, are affected by paragraph formats. Paragraph formats *do not just affect* single characters, words, or sentences.

Paragraph marks (¶) indicate where a paragraph ends

Note that while all these paragraphs in this screenshot of a Word document have the same character formats (they are all in the same font, size, and so on) they still appear different, because their paragraph formats are different

This·is·a·left-aligned·paragraph.¶

This·is·a·right-aligned·paragraph.¶

This·is·a·centred·paragraph.¶

This·paragraph·has·single·line-spacing·and·is·indented·by·a· small·amount·on·its·first·line.·Lines·are·close·together,·set·by· Word·itself.·This·is·a·standard·setting·unless·you·change·the· default·style·(covered·later·in·the·book).¶

This·paragraph·has·double·line-spacing·and·is·indented·

on·its·first·line·by·a·slightly·larger·amount.·Lines·are·obviously·

wider·apart·than·the·previous·paragraph.·It's·possible·to·do·this·

all·in·Word·quite·simply·when·you·know·what·you're·doing.¶

Paragraph marks (¶) are used by Word to store a paragraph's formatting

Take note:

A paragraph is defined as any block of text — no matter how short, or how long — ending with a paragraph mark ¶. A paragraph mark is added to your text each time you press `Enter` or ⏎.

Paragraph marks *may* be hidden — to display them (or hide them if they are currently displayed) click the Show/Hide ¶ button ¶ on the Standard toolbar

Basic steps:

1 First select the paragraph or paragraphs you intend to format

2 Apply the new paragraph format or formats

To apply a paragraph format to a paragraph you use the same techniques you use to apply a character format to a character.

> 1 Select the paragraph or paragraphs (in this example there are two paragraphs) you want to format

Here we go, here we go, here we go. It's another fine, fine day down at the ranch. The brunch is cooking and the horses are lively. After we've eaten we'll get going and round-up the cattle. Never in the field of human conflict has so much been eaten by so few. ¶
Inevitably, there will be a cut in resources. There's now so little money to go round that it's just a question of jobs or the tools to do those jobs. If we want to maintain current levels of employment, we'll all just have to do with less to spend. ¶

Take note:

You don't have to select a whole paragraph before you apply paragraph formatting to it. If you position the insertion point *anywhere* within the paragraph then apply paragraph formatting the *entire* paragraph is formatted

Tip:

If you are currently typing text into a formatted paragraph, then press Enter or ⏎, the new paragraph so created continues with the format of the preceding paragraph. In other words, if you have formatted a paragraph to the paragraph style you want, each subsequent paragraph has the same format

> 2 Apply the paragraph formats – here the paragraphs have been indented on their first lines and justified

Here we go, here we go, here we go. It's another fine, fine day down at the ranch. The brunch is cooking and the horses are lively. After we've eaten we'll get going and round-up the cattle. Never in the field of human conflict has so much been eaten by so few. ¶
Inevitably, there will be a cut in resources. There's now so little money to go round that it's just a question of jobs or the tools to do those jobs. If we want to maintain current levels of employment, we'll all just have to do with less to spend. ¶

Paragraph formats (contd)

Like character formats, paragraph formats can be applied to text in three main ways.

Justify button

Right align button

Centre align button

Left align button

1 The Formatting toolbar, shown with the ruler

Button to increase indent from the left margin

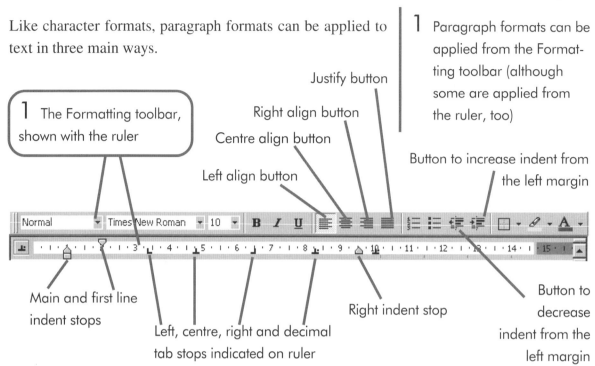

Main and first line indent stops

Left, centre, right and decimal tab stops indicated on ruler

Right indent stop

Button to decrease indent from the left margin

Tip:

Unlike some word processors, Word does not use formatting codes. The formats you apply are visible directly on-screen, so you can see what they will print like. If, however, you want to see the particular paragraph (or character) formats applied, first choose Help ⤷What's This?, or type Shift + F1, then click in the paragraph.

A Paragraph Formatting dialog box is displayed which shows the formatting applied. Click 🔲 again, or press ⎋ to get rid of it

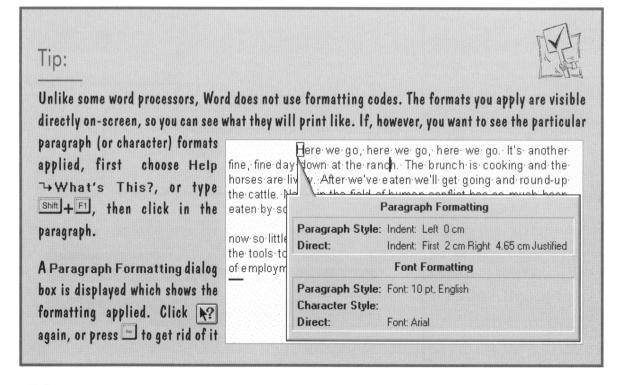

Here we go, here we go, here we go. It's another fine, fine day down at the ranch. The brunch is cooking and the horses are lively. After we've eaten we'll get going and round-up the cattle. No in the field of human conflict has so much been eaten by so

now so little the tools to of employm

Paragraph Formatting

| **Paragraph Style:** | Indent: Left 0 cm |
| **Direct:** | Indent: First 2 cm Right 4.65 cm Justified |

Font Formatting

Paragraph Style:	Font: 10 pt, English
Character Style:	
Direct:	Font: Arial

2 Formats can be applied from the **Paragraph** dialog box (to display it choose **Format** ↳ **Paragraph**, or type Alt + O then P)

contd…

2 The **Paragraph** dialog box, from which many paragraph formatting options can be set as one step

Click this tab for special text flow options (see over)

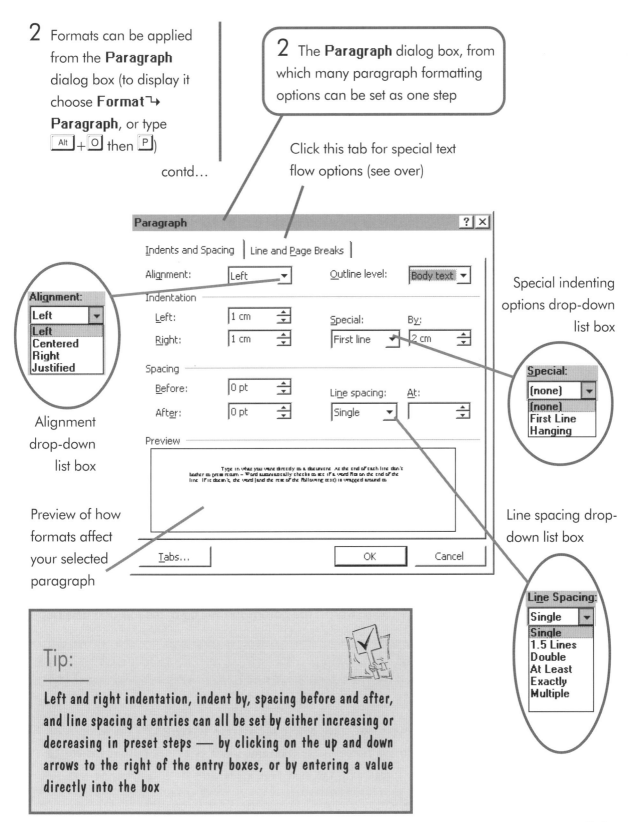

Alignment drop-down list box

Special indenting options drop-down list box

Preview of how formats affect your selected paragraph

Line spacing drop-down list box

Tip:

Left and right indentation, indent by, spacing before and after, and line spacing at entries can all be set by either increasing or decreasing in preset steps — by clicking on the up and down arrows to the right of the entry boxes, or by entering a value directly into the box

Paragraph formats (contd)

Special paragraph formatting attributes are available from the **Text Flow** tab option of the **Paragraph** dialog box. These attributes directly affect the way text flows between pages of a document. Main ones are labelled and described.

Checking this prevents a paragraph from being split from the following paragraph

Checking this check box prevents the last line of a paragraph from being printed at the top of a page (a widow), or the first line of a paragraph from being printed alone at the bottom of a page (an orphan)

Checking this prevents a paragraph being split across pages at all

Checking this inserts a page break before a paragraph (in other words, the paragraph will be at the top of a new page)

Tip:

These attributes can make a document look much better and prevent anomalies. If the Keep with Next option is checked for a paragraph formatted as a heading which by chance falls at the bottom of a page, for example, it will be forced onto the next page along with its accompanying text

Basic steps contd:

3 Paragraph formats can be applied directly with keyboard shortcut combinations. Like character formatting keyboard combinations, these are very often the quickest ways of applying certain formats

KEYBOARD SHORTCUT COMBINATIONS

Left-align text	`Ctrl` + `B`
Centre align text	`Ctrl` + `E`
Right-align text	`Ctrl` + `R`
Justify text	`Ctrl` + `J`
Indent from left margin	`Ctrl` + `M`
Decrease indent	`Ctrl` + `Shift` + `M`
Create a hanging indent	`Ctrl` + `T`
Decrease a hanging indent	`Ctrl` + `Shift` + `T`
1 line space	`Ctrl` + `1`
1.5 line space	`Ctrl` + `5`
2 line space	`Ctrl` + `2`
Add or remove 12 points of space before a paragraph	`Ctrl` + `0`
Remove paragraph formats not applied by a style	`Ctrl` + `Q`
Restore Normal style	`Ctrl` + `Shift` + `N`
Display or hide nonprinting characters (¶ and so on)	`Ctrl` + `*`

Tip:

You can quickly indent selected paragraphs using either the keyboard shortcut combinations above right, or (better) using the Decrease or Increase indent buttons on the Formatting toolbar.

While changes due to these methods are in fixed increments (0.5 inch by default) you can always later change them by dragging indent markers on the ruler

Take note:

While character and paragraph formats are all very nice, and very good, and used properly can greatly improve the look of a document, bear in mind you have to apply every one of them individually.

On the other hand, you can apply formats automatically by using styles (page 120). Automatic formatting is much quicker and, because you can use both methods across documents, ensures that documents you create can have a unified style, or set of styles, giving a much more professional appearance to your work

Tabs

Any word processor has the ability to define tab stops. These are used to help align text, such that tables or columns of figures, say, can be neatened up and aligned underneath each other.

Word has several types of tab stops, which allow text to be aligned in a number of ways:

● left-aligned — with text aligned after the tab stop

● centre-aligned — with text centred around the tab stop

● right-aligned — where text is aligned-right to the tab stop

● decimal-aligned — with columns of monetary figures, say, aligned so their decimal point is align directly on the tab stop

● bar-aligned — Word creates a vertical line in your document, the height of the text line, at the tab stop.

Tabs are inserted into the ruler in force above a paragraph. They then apply to all the lines within the paragraph.

The various tab types are shown below.

Basic steps:

The most straightforward way of setting tabs is with the ruler:

1 Repeatedly click the Tab Alignment button (preset as) until the type of tab you require is displayed

   L — align left

   ⊥ — align centre

   ⌐ — align right

   ⊥ — align to decimal point

2 Click in the ruler at the position you want the tab stop. It is displayed in the ruler as a symbol, according to which tab stop type you selected

3 Adjust the tab stop if you need, by dragging it along the ruler to its new position

Take note:

Tabs are paragraph formats. In other words, they are set for and remain in force for a paragraph — no matter how many lines the paragraph runs to

Take note:

As you insert a new tab stop, any default tab stops to its left disappear

1 The Tab Alignment button – keep clicking it until the tab stop you want is selected (align left is default)

`L ⎥ · I · 1 ⌐ I · 2 · I · 3 ⊥ I · 4 · I · 5 ⌐ I · 6 · I · 7 ⊥ I · 8 · I · 9 ⎥ I · 10 · I · 11 · I · 12 · I · 13 · I · 14 · I ⎤ 15 · I ·`

2 After selecting a tab stop type, click in the ruler to position your tab stop. The tab stop is displayed by one of four symbols (plus the bar tab symbol)

Old tab position   New tab position

`L ⎥ · I · 1 · I · ⎧2 · I · 3 ⊥ I · 4 · I · 5 ⌐ I · 6 · I · 7 ⊥ I · 8 · I · 9 ⎥ I · 10 · I · 11 · I · 12 · I · 13 · I · 14 · I ⎤ 15 · I ·`

¶

As you drag, a line shows you the new tab position in the document

3 You can adjust a tab stop's position by dragging it along the ruler to where you want it

59

Simple tables

To tabulate a simple table you can use tabs. Because tabs are a paragraph format, you need to select the paragraphs which form the table before setting the tabs — in exactly the same ways described when we selected text previously. Once the paragraphs forming the table are selected, the tab changes you make affect all those paragraphs.

2 Set your tabs (don't worry if they're not exact – just set them approximately)

3 Adjust the tabs (by dragging them along the ruler to suit) until the text tabulates as you want – by typing text in first using the default tab stops, followed by setting your own tabs then adjusting them, you can see the effects of adjustment on-screen

4 Make any changes to character or other paragraph formats you want

---

Take note:

Never press ⌨Tab more than once to align text. It doesn't matter if text doesn't align as you want while you're entering it (see Tip below) — it's still better to change the tabs later to suit your layout requirements. That way you can see the effects of changes you make to the text directly. If you set the tab stops *before* you enter the text, you're just guessing where they need to be, and you'll almost certainly have to change them anyway!

Tip:

Don't bother setting tabs before you start to type text into a new document. The default tabs in a Word document (set at every half inch — or 1.27 centimetre) will let you tabulate the text initially (it probably won't align at all as you type it in — but don't worry). Once the text is completely entered you can select it, then put the tab stops where you want. Even once you've set the tab stops you can change them to suit, until you've got the text looking as you want it

1 Select the paragraphs you want – note the heading of the table isn't selected here

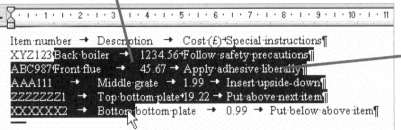

Note how the default tab stops render the table some-what unattractive – it doesn't matter at this stage because step 3 tidies it up

2 Set the tabs you want for each column of the table (see pages 60—61)

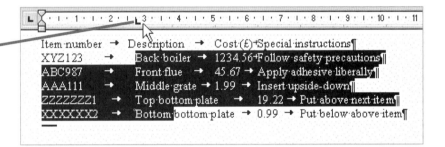

3 Adjust the tabs to suit the table and the appearance you want

Now the heading can be tabulated to suit

4 Make character and other paragraph formatting changes you want

61

More about tabs

While the ruler affords by far the easiest method of setting and adjusting tabs, it is actually quite inexact and some tab options aren't available from it. Total control over tabs (both setting and adjusting) is available from the **Tabs** dialog box.

Tip:

A quick way to display the Tabs dialog box is to double-click a tab in the ruler

Basic steps:

1 Display the **Tabs** dialog box by choosing **Format ↳ Tabs** or by typing `Alt` + `O` then `T` (or by clicking the **Tabs** button in the **Paragraph** dialog box – see page 55)

2 Set tab stop positions, alignment types, and leaders (if required)

Change default tab stop spacing for a document from here

1 **Tabs** dialog box

2 Set:
- tab positions
- alignment types
- leaders

to suit

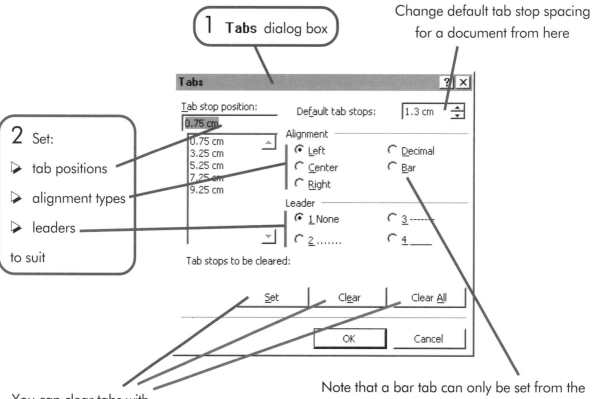

You can clear tabs with these buttons, or set those you enter

Note that a bar tab can only be set from the **Tabs** dialog box – not from the ruler (although you can adjust it – once set – from the ruler)

There are two ways you can clear tabs:

- ❏ You can use the clear buttons in the **Tabs** dialog box (see opposite)

- ❏ You can literally drag the tabs off the ruler so they disappear. This is by far the faster method where only a few tabs are to be cleared

Tip:

Tabs — as we've already seen — are paragraph formats. Like all the other paragraph formats they remain in operation after each paragraph, until you change them.

If you want tab settings to remain in operation for a few paragraphs you can set them before you start, then type away. As you press Enter or ⏎ to begin a new paragraph the formats (including tab settings) are carried over

Tip:

You can fill the empty space before a tab stop with dotted, dashed, or solid lines called leaders. They can give a professional finish to contents pages, say, where a contents list is separated from its page number list by some considerable space

Take note:

You can only set or clear leaders from the Tabs dialog box

Borders and shading

Two other paragraph formats which can be used to create a professional appearance to Word documents are paragraph borders and shading.

Borders are rules around a paragraph (which may, or may not, be thick enough to see — a border of zero thickness is still there, albeit not visible). Shadings are the background shades of colours or greys which go inside borders.

Borders are set up and adjusted in one of three ways:

● with the Borders button on the Formatting toolbar

● through the Tables & Borders toolbar

● with the **Paragraph Borders and Shading** dialog box.

The best way to apply borders and shading is with the Tables & Borders toolbar

1 If it's not already displayed, call up the Tables & Borders toolbar (by right-clicking any toolbar and checking the **Tables & Borders** checkbox)

How the paragraph is formatted is very important to how the bordered and shaded paragraph will look. Justified or centred text always looks better than left- or right-aligned text, simply because the borders (and resultant shading) are evenly placed around the text

Borders can be:

▷ thinner

▷ thicker

▷ nonexistent

> Here is a bordered paragraph — I think it looks really smart. If text is justified — which this is, or centred, it gives a tidy appearance at each side.

> Here is another bordered paragraph — this time though aligned left to see the difference. Not so good, hmm? I agree. However, what do you think of the shading?

> Here is a paragraph with no border but some shading. As the shading is quite dark (60%) the text colour has been reversed to white creating a nice effect.

For a paragraph you intend to shade darkly, consider reversing text to create a pleasant effect

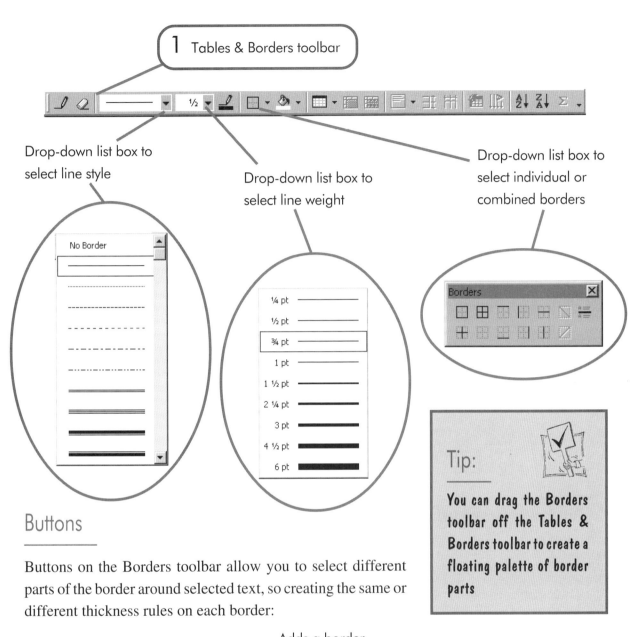

Drop-down list box to select line style

Drop-down list box to select line weight

Drop-down list box to select individual or combined borders

No Border

¼ pt
½ pt
¾ pt
1 pt
1 ½ pt
2 ¼ pt
3 pt
4 ½ pt
6 pt

Borders

Tip:

You can drag the Borders toolbar off the Tables & Borders toolbar to create a floating palette of border parts

Buttons

Buttons on the Borders toolbar allow you to select different parts of the border around selected text, so creating the same or different thickness rules on each border:

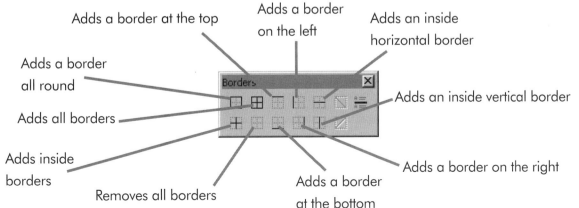

Adds a border at the top

Adds a border on the left

Adds an inside horizontal border

Adds a border all round

Adds all borders

Borders

Adds an inside vertical border

Adds inside borders

Adds a border on the right

Removes all borders

Adds a border at the bottom

Borders & shading (contd)

When you add a border to text it extends around the full size of the paragraph the text is formatted to. In other words, whatever the width and height of the paragraph will be the width and height of the border — regardless of whether the text itself totally fills the border. This can result in unusual (and probably unattractive) borders.

1 Select the text to have a border – remember (as borders and shades are paragraph formats) you only need to click in the paragraph to select the whole paragraph

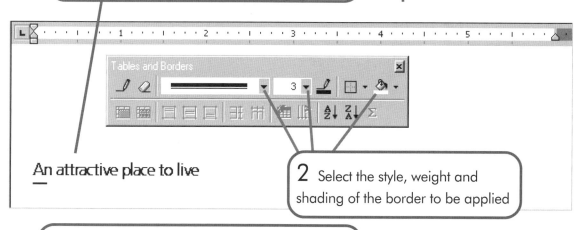

An attractive place to live

2 Select the style, weight and shading of the border to be applied

3 Apply the border – this one is a boxed border, applied with the boxed border button

An attractive place to live

4 Drag the right indent marker of the ruler in, until the indent is just to the right of the text in the paragraph

The paragraph is now boxed properly and attractively – note that if you now add to the text in the bordered paragraph the border will still be the correct width as the text simply overflows onto the next line which is of the same width. The border's bottom rule remains below the bottom line of the paragraph however many lines it has

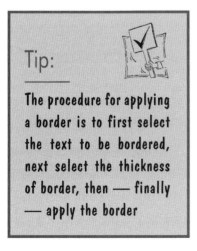

Tip:

The procedure for applying a border is to first select the text to be bordered, next select the thickness of border, then — finally — apply the border

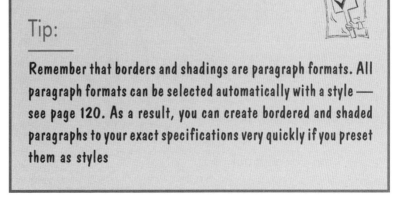

Tip:

Remember that borders and shadings are paragraph formats. All paragraph formats can be selected automatically with a style — see page 120. As a result, you can create bordered and shaded paragraphs to your exact specifications very quickly if you preset them as styles

67

Borders & shading (contd)

You can create and adjust borders and shadings through the **Borders and Shading** dialog box too. While this isn't as quick as using the Borders toolbar it does provide some options not otherwise available.

1 The **Borders and Shading** dialog box

Click this tab to see the shading options

Preview

Some borders are preset – just click the one you want

Choose the colours of borders from this drop-down list box

Click here to specify that a border is spaced a greater distance from the edges of text (default is 1 point – a typo-graphical measurement which is about 1/72 of an inch)

Click this tab to get back to borders options

You can display the Borders toolbar (if it's not already displayed) by clicking this button

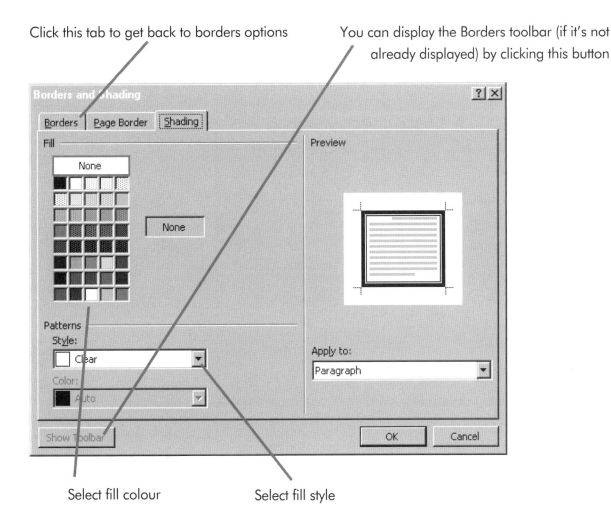

Select fill colour

Select fill style

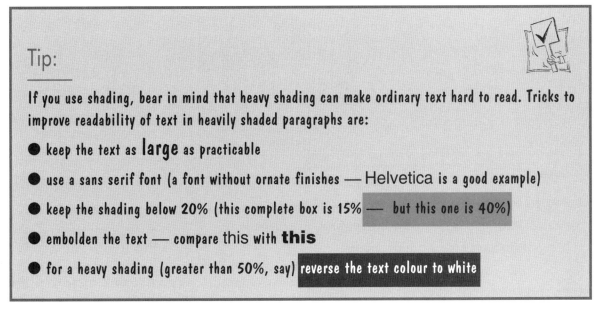

Tip:

If you use shading, bear in mind that heavy shading can make ordinary text hard to read. Tricks to improve readability of text in heavily shaded paragraphs are:

● keep the text as large as practicable

● use a sans serif font (a font without ornate finishes — Helvetica is a good example)

● keep the shading below 20% (this complete box is 15% — but this one is 40%)

● embolden the text — compare this with **this**

● for a heavy shading (greater than 50%, say) reverse the text colour to white

Summary

❑ Both character and paragraph formatting are useful –
apply them to selected text by all means – but automatic
formatting (using Word styles – covered in Chapter 6) is
even more useful.

❑ Formatting – whether character formats, paragraph formats or styles – is the key to producing good-looking
effective documents.

❑ Character and paragraph formats are quickly applied by
clicking buttons on the Formatting toolbar – keyboard
shortcuts, however, are often even quicker

❑ If you apply a format to the insertion point, the format
continues as you type until you change it again.

❑ If a format already exists in your document, and you want to
use it again, use the Format Painter button ✎ on the
Standard toolbar to paint the format wherever you want.

❑ Paragraph formats are all stored in a paragraph's paragraph marker ¶.

❑ Don't bother setting tabs before you enter text – let Word's
default tabs do the work for you until you've typed in the text
you want to be tabulated. After you've typed it in, select the
text then set and adjust your tab to suit.

❑ Set and adjust tabs from the ruler wherever possible – this
is by far the quickest way.

❑ Use borders and shading to emphasise points in your
document.

❑ Borders (and shading) extends right around the text block –
to each indent. If you want the border around just the text,
bring the indents in to those positions.

4 Sections and pages

About sections

Sometimes when you are working on a document, you need to split it up into smaller parts, without splitting it up into totally different documents. These smaller parts are called *sections*.

You only need to create sections if you want to change the appearance of parts of your document in certain ways. The changes you can make within a document which require that sections have to be created include:

● a different page size

● different margins (page 75)

● a different number of columns (page 84)

● a different header or footer (page 78)

● different line numberings (page 82).

In normal view (and in print layout view if the Show/Hide ¶ button ¶ on the Standard toolbar is clicked), a section end is displayed as shown below.

Take note:

You only need to split your document up into sections if *part* of your document needs to have one or more of these changes applied. If the *whole* document needs to have the change applied there's no need to use sections at all

A section break, indicated by a dotted line. This does not print

---

The quiet revolution
The personal computer world is in a state of limbo as Intel's domination of the market is about to be challenged.

··Section Break (Next Page)··

Things move pretty quickly where personal computers are concerned. From the dawn of the personal computer era just twelve years ago several generations of integrated circuits have come and gone, tens of computer manufacturers have made fortunes and bitten the dust, and just a handful of manufacturers now seems to survive. But that's by no means an end to the story. This year there's the start of what will come to be seen as the biggest shake-up ever know in the industry, with conventions overthrown and market percentages re-negotiated to an extent never seen before. Yet users could be forgiven for not even realizing what's going on. Most of the changes have occurred so far in the mainstream background, with little noise and a great deal of stealth.

Basic steps:

1 Position the insertion point in your document where you want the new section to be, then choose **Insert⇥Break**, or type `Alt`+`I` then `B`, to call up the **Break** dialog box

2 Click the button corresponding to the section break you want:

❏ **Next Page** – the section break causes the document to force following text to appear at the top of the next page

❏ **Continuous** – following text occurs straight under the section break, wherever it occurs on a page

❏ **Even Page** – following text is forced to the top of the next even page of the document

❏ **Odd page** – following text is forced to the top of the next odd page of the document

3 Click **OK**

Effectively, the changes listed are parameters you apply much like character and paragraph formats, except they affect the whole section (not just a few characters or paragraphs). Every time you want to change one or more of these parameters in just *part* of your document, you need a new section.

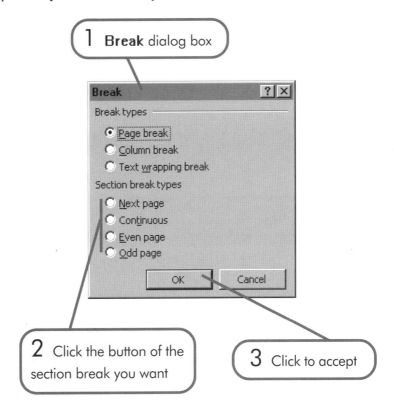

1 **Break** dialog box

2 Click the button of the section break you want

3 Click to accept

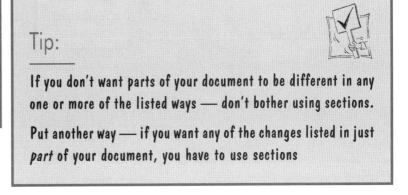

Tip:

If you don't want parts of your document to be different in any one or more of the listed ways — don't bother using sections.

Put another way — if you want any of the changes listed in just *part* of your document, you have to use sections

Setting up a document

Apart from character and paragraph formats, a document has other parameters you can format. Where these are contained within a section (or selected sections) of a document they affect just that section (or sections). Where the document contains no section breaks (that is, the document comprises just one section), or where all sections of a document are selected before formatting, the whole document is affected.

Most of these parameters are adjusted from the **Page Setup** dialog box, although other methods are sometimes available.

1 Choose **File→Page Setup**, or type [Alt]+[F] then [U], to call up the **Page Setup** dialog box

2 Click tabs to see the different controls available to adjust parameters

3 If you make any changes to parameters, click **OK** to accept changes, or **Cancel** to ignore them

1 **Page Setup** dialog box

2 Tabs allow different controls to be adjusted. Click tabs to bring those controls frontmost in the dialog box

Preview of your document's overall appearance with parameters as you set them in the dialog box

3 Accept or ignore your changes

Basic steps:

1 Choose **File→Page Setup**, or type `Alt`+`F` then `U`, to call up the **Page Setup** dialog box

2 Click the **Margins** tab if it's not already frontmost (see opposite)

3 Adjust margin dimensions to suit

Margins are imaginary guides on a document page, outside of which text isn't normally situated. By default, Word creates margins for any new document — usually of 1 inch (2.54 cm) from top and bottom of the page, and 1.25 inches (3.17 cm) from left and right page edge.

You can change margins, either for a whole document or for a section, from the **Page Setup** dialog box.

Tip:

In many of these tabs (and in many other dialog boxes, for that matter) adjustments can be made to some controls by increasing or decreasing in preset steps by clicking up or down arrows to the right of the entry boxes. Alternatively, you can click on the entry box you want to change then enter the exact value you want

Tip:

You can specify that the margin changes be applied to just the section you are in, from the current point on (Word places a section break at the insertion point and changes apply to the section following it), or the whole document, from the drop-down list box on the Margins tab of the Page Setup dialog box

Apply To: | This Section ▼

This Section
This Point Forward
Whole Document

Margins (contd)

Some of the controls of the **Margins** tab of the **Page Setup** dialog box allow you to control how pages are printed for double-sided purposes (that is, for the likes of books and reports).

If the document is to be double-sided, check the **Mirror Margins** check box

Change the **Inside** and **Outside** margins measurements to suit your requirements

If you plan to bind your document with a ring or similar method, enter a value in the **Gutter** entry box – this adds space to the margins to allow for the binding

2 If the **Mirror Margins** check box is checked, these entry boxes change to show **Inside** and **Outside** margin measurements

Preview always shows the effects of entries and controls

3 Entering a value here creates an extra space to allow for a binding

1 Check here for margins which are equal on the inside and outside of left and right hand pages, or top and bottom of above and below pages

Basic steps:

Rapid margin adjustment

DRAG ADJUSTMENT

1 Choose **View**⤷**Print layout**, or type [Alt]+[V] then [P], or (best) click the print layout button 🗏 to view your document in print layout view

2 Drag your margins to suit

As an alternative to using the **Page Setup** dialog box, you can adjust margins by dragging margin boundaries in print layout view. This is probably faster, though you have little accuracy, you can't specify how much of the document you want to apply changes to (current section, current point forward, or the whole document — dragging from the ruler applies changes to just the current section, or whole document if no section break exists), and mirror margin and gutter margin controls aren't available.

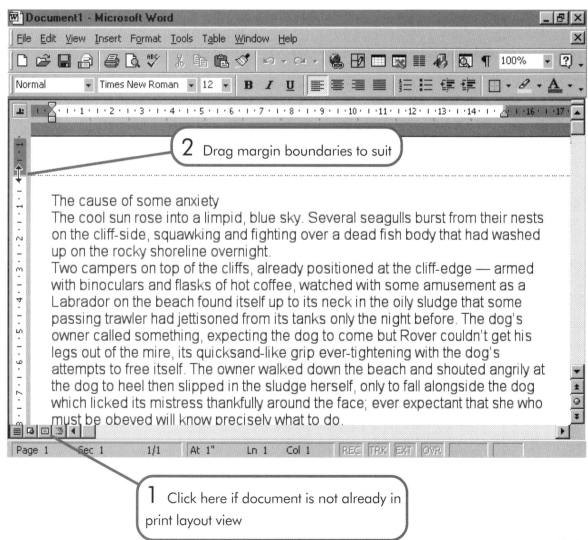

2 Drag margin boundaries to suit

The cause of some anxiety
The cool sun rose into a limpid, blue sky. Several seagulls burst from their nests on the cliff-side, squawking and fighting over a dead fish body that had washed up on the rocky shoreline overnight.
Two campers on top of the cliffs, already positioned at the cliff-edge — armed with binoculars and flasks of hot coffee, watched with some amusement as a Labrador on the beach found itself up to its neck in the oily sludge that some passing trawler had jettisoned from its tanks only the night before. The dog's owner called something, expecting the dog to come but Rover couldn't get his legs out of the mire, its quicksand-like grip ever-tightening with the dog's attempts to free itself. The owner walked down the beach and shouted angrily at the dog to heel then slipped in the sludge herself, only to fall alongside the dog which licked its mistress thankfully around the face; ever expectant that she who must be obeyed will know precisely what to do.

1 Click here if document is not already in print layout view

Headers and footers

A header is a heading (often called a running head) which appears at the top of each page in a document or section of a document. A footer is at the bottom of each page. You can put text or graphical items in either and you can format them in the usual ways.

Basic steps:

1 To create either a header or a footer choose **View→Header and Footer**, or type ⌊Alt⌋+⌊V⌋ then ⌊H⌋. The document changes to print layout view and displays the header entry box and the Header and Footer toolbar

Tip:

Headers and footers apply to individual sections — in other words, you can have different headers and footers for each section if you want

Tip:

Your document's text is displayed grey when in Headers and Footers view. Double-click anywhere in the text, however, and the text becomes active (sending the headers and footers to a greyed background outline). You can switch between the two by double-clicking each in this way

Double-click a greyed header to make it active

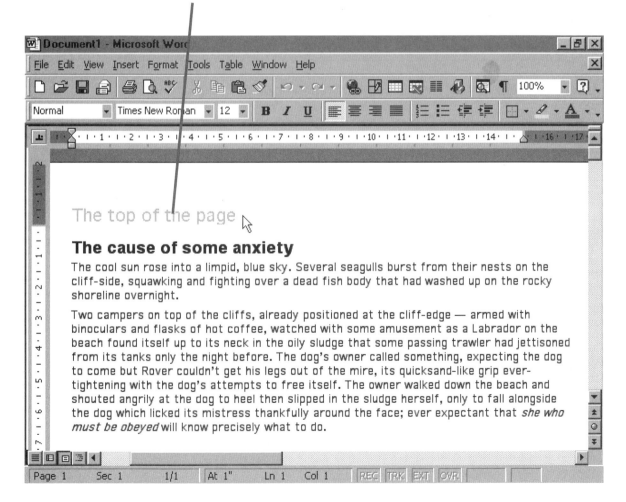

The cause of some anxiety

The cool sun rose into a limpid, blue sky. Several seagulls burst from their nests on the cliff-side, squawking and fighting over a dead fish body that had washed up on the rocky shoreline overnight.

Two campers on top of the cliffs, already positioned at the cliff-edge — armed with binoculars and flasks of hot coffee, watched with some amusement as a Labrador on the beach found itself up to its neck in the oily sludge that some passing trawler had jettisoned from its tanks only the night before. The dog's owner called something, expecting the dog to come but Rover couldn't get his legs out of the mire, its quicksand-like grip ever-tightening with the dog's attempts to free itself. The owner walked down the beach and shouted angrily at the dog to heel then slipped in the sludge herself, only to fall alongside the dog which licked its mistress thankfully around the face; ever expectant that *she who must be obeyed* will know precisely what to do.

Headers & footers (contd)

The Headers and Footers toolbar has a number of buttons. Use these to access various features and entries you can make into a header or footer.

Switch Between Header and Footer button – click to move from a header to a footer or back (alternatively, you can scroll down or up the page in the document window)

Show/Hide Document Text button – jumps between document text and header or footer text

Page Setup button – calls up the **Page Setup** dialog box

Close – click when you no longer need the Headers and Footers toolbar

Current Date, and Current Time

Page Number, Insert Number of Pages, Format Page Number

Show Previous and Show Next buttons – click either to jump to the next header or footer in your document (you can only do this if you have different headers or footers – in other words you have to have other sections with other headers or footers set up)

Same As Previous button – allows you to delete an existing, or create a new, header or footer

Tip:

Remember you can format a header or a footer in exactly the same way you format ordinary document text. You can embolden, italicise, underline and so on. You can make it centrally aligned or right aligned if you want. You are not restricted to just one line of text. You can also use a graphical item.

Also remember that each section you create can have its own header and footer — use this feature to set up a header for each chapter of a large document, for example

Basic steps:

1 Choose **View �’Print layout**, or type `Alt`+`V` then `P`, or (best) click the Print Layout button ▤ to view your document in print layout view

2 Drag margin and header (or footer) boundaries to suit

You can adjust the distance from a page edge taken up by a header at the top of your document page (or the footer at the bottom) from the **Page Setup** dialog box (the **From Edge** entries). You can also change margins from here (allowing you to adjust the distance between the header or footer and the document text).

An easier way, however, is to switch to print layout view and drag the various boundaries to suit what you want.

Line numbers

Word can display and print line numbers alongside text. This can be useful in technical documentation, and even required in legal literature.

Line numbers are:

● printed in the left margin

● numbered excluding lines in tables, headers, footers and some other parts of a document

● only visible on-screen in print layout view (or print preview — see page 140).

— see page 140).

Basic steps:

1 Choose **File↳Page Setup**, or type [Alt]+[F] then [U] to call up the **Page Setup** dialog box. Click the **Layout** tab if it's not already frontmost. Next click the **Line Numbers** button to call up the **Line Numbers** dialog box

2 Check the **Add Line Numbering** check box to create line numbers

3 Adjust controls to suit and click **OK** to accept and view line numbers

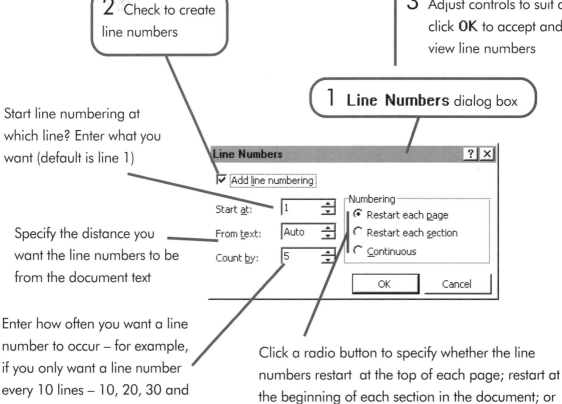

2 Check to create line numbers

Start line numbering at which line? Enter what you want (default is line 1)

1 Line Numbers dialog box

Specify the distance you want the line numbers to be from the document text

Enter how often you want a line number to occur – for example, if you only want a line number every 10 lines – 10, 20, 30 and so on – enter 10

Click a radio button to specify whether the line numbers restart at the top of each page; restart at the beginning of each section in the document; or are continuous throughout

82

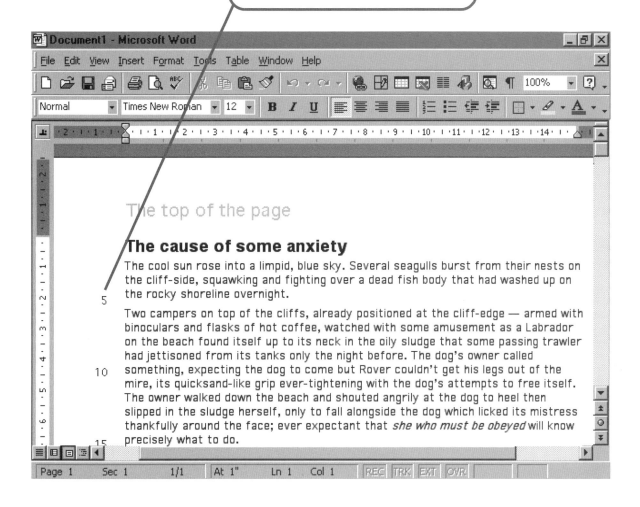

3 Line numbers are visible in print layout (or print preview) views only

The top of the page

The cause of some anxiety

The cool sun rose into a limpid, blue sky. Several seagulls burst from their nests on the cliff-side, squawking and fighting over a dead fish body that had washed up on the rocky shoreline overnight.

5

Two campers on top of the cliffs, already positioned at the cliff-edge — armed with binoculars and flasks of hot coffee, watched with some amusement as a Labrador on the beach found itself up to its neck in the oily sludge that some passing trawler had jettisoned from its tanks only the night before. The dog's owner called something, expecting the dog to come but Rover couldn't get his legs out of the mire, its quicksand-like grip ever-tightening with the dog's attempts to free itself. The owner walked down the beach and shouted angrily at the dog to heel then slipped in the sludge herself, only to fall alongside the dog which licked its mistress thankfully around the face; ever expectant that *she who must be obeyed* will know precisely what to do.

10

15

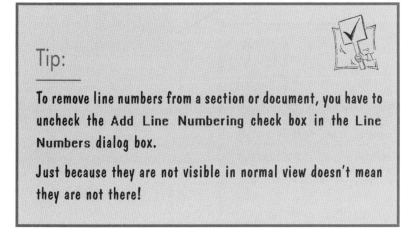

Tip:

To remove line numbers from a section or document, you have to uncheck the Add Line Numbering check box in the Line Numbers dialog box.

Just because they are not visible in normal view doesn't mean they are not there!

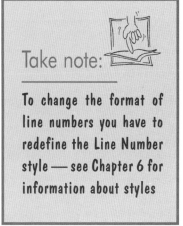

Take note:

To change the format of line numbers you have to redefine the Line Number style — see Chapter 6 for information about styles

Columns

Generally, text in a Word document is in a single column — that is, a single vertical division down the page. You can, however, create two or more columns of text quite simply, where columns are unattached or where a story flows from the bottom of one column to the top of the next. Columns can be used to create newspaper-style or newsletter-style documents, or indeed books such as this one.

You can create columns in your document from either:

● a button on the Standard toolbar; or

● the **Columns** dialog box.

USING THE STANDARD TOOLBAR

1 Select the text you want to be formatted into columns, then click the Columns button on the Standard toolbar

2 Drag across the drop-down window to select the number of columns you want

Click the Columns button to display this drop-down window

Drag across to select the number of columns you want – let go the mouse button to accept

Take note:

You can only see columns you create in print layout view or print preview view (see page 140)! In normal view, text is simply displayed at the width of a *single* column — so if your text is across two columns on the page, normally viewed text will only be a half page wide

Basic steps:

FROM THE COLUMNS DIALOG BOX

1 Select the text you want to be formatted into columns, then choose **Format ↪Columns** to call up the **Columns** dialog box, or type `Alt`+`F`, then `C`

2 Choose the number of columns you want

3 Change column widths and other controls to suit your requirements

Tip:

If you select text then format it into columns, Word then automatically inserts section breaks before and after the text. This way you can have different numbers of columns in different parts of the document — columns are section parameters, remember.

If you simply position the insertion point in your document before formatting into columns (that is, you *don't* select any text), the whole section (the whole *document* if no section breaks are present in the document) is formatted

1 **Columns** dialog box

2 Click to select the number of columns from these buttons, or enter the number in the lower box

3 Adjust column widths to suit

Specify which part of document to apply columns to (whole document, current section, or from this point on)

Columns (contd)

If you want to format your section or document into even-width columns, the quickest method is with the Columns button on the Standard toolbar.

On the other hand, if you want *uneven* columns you have to use the **Columns** dialog box. The **Columns** dialog box also gives some other controls unavailable with the Columns button:

● the spacing between columns

● whether a line between columns is displayed

● whether the columns apply to the whole document, the current section, or from the current point on.

Tip:

If you want multi-column text underneath single column text first enter text without any column for-matting. Next, select the text to be multi-column formatted and format it. Word automatically cre-ates section breaks before and after the multi-column formatted section

Click here to give two columns of unequal width – measurements in the width entry boxes are automatically adjusted to suit

Check this box to create a line between columns

Click here to maintain equal-width columns – all measure-ments are automatically adjusted

Preview shows you the effects of changing controls

Tip:

You can adjust column widths and the spaces between them by dragging boundaries on the rulers in print layout or print preview views, as shown below. This is often quicker and simpler than from the Columns dialog box, but less accurate

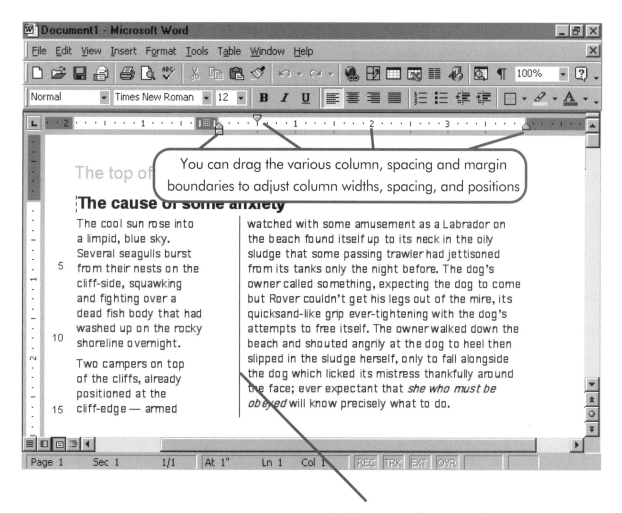

You can drag the various column, spacing and margin boundaries to adjust column widths, spacing, and positions

The cause of some anxiety

The cool sun rose into a limpid, blue sky. Several seagulls burst from their nests on the cliff-side, squawking and fighting over a dead fish body that had washed up on the rocky shoreline overnight.

Two campers on top of the cliffs, already positioned at the cliff-edge — armed

watched with some amusement as a Labrador on the beach found itself up to its neck in the oily sludge that some passing trawler had jettisoned from its tanks only the night before. The dog's owner called something, expecting the dog to come but Rover couldn't get his legs out of the mire, its quicksand-like grip ever-tightening with the dog's attempts to free itself. The owner walked down the beach and shouted angrily at the dog to heel then slipped in the sludge herself, only to fall alongside the dog which licked its mistress thankfully around the face; ever expectant that *she who must be obeyed* will know precisely what to do.

Line between columns

Summary

❑ Use a section where you need to change certain parameters for only part of your document. The parameters for which a section has to be created include:

  ▷ a different page size

  ▷ different margins

  ▷ a different number of columns

  ▷ a different header or footer

  ▷ different line numberings.

❑ If you change any of these parameters for the whole document, don't use a section.

❑ Create margins, headers and footers, and columns from dialog boxes (as this is most exact), but remember you can adjust them and their spacings by dragging boundaries in print layout (or print preview) view.

5 Text control

Finding text

Although it probably sounds odd, one of the main jobs a word processor is asked to do in everyday life is to find text. You'd think a word processor had enough coping with all it's asked to do with text without having to actually find the stuff for you too, wouldn't you?

Problem is, in long documents it's not always easy for us to locate specific instances of small pieces of text. Let's say you have worked for weeks and weeks on your latest novel, and you decide that little bit around half way through about your heroine's need for money needs expanding somewhat. What do you do? You could scroll through the book, screen-by-screen, trying to find where it is, but that could take hours — you wrote it weeks ago remember — and you haven't a real idea exactly where it is.

Let Word do the job for you.

1. Choose **Edit**↪**Find**, or type [Alt] + [E] then [F], or type [Ctrl] + [F]. This calls up the **Find and Replace** dialog box

2. In the **Find what** entry box, type in the text you want to locate

3. If your text contains formats, special characters or other controls, click the **More** button to extend the dialog box

4. Specify the controls you want to control the search

5. Click the **Find Next** button to start the search

2 The text you want to find

1 **Find** dialog box

Find and Replace ? X

Find | Replace | Go To

Find what: | This is a hold-up, gimme the money | ▼

More ∓ | Find Next | Cancel

3 Click if things other than just text can be specified

90

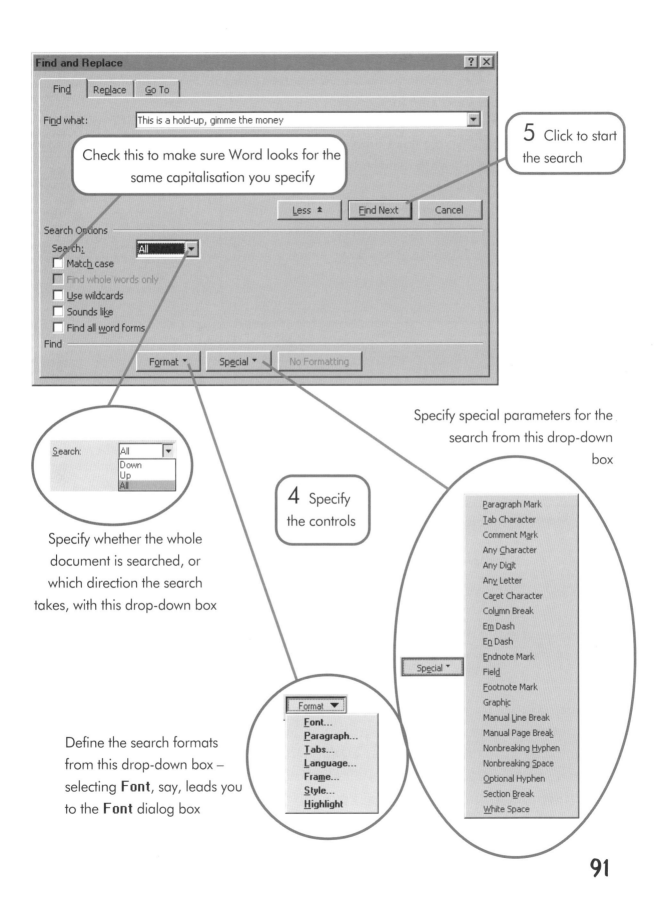

Find and Replace

Find | Replace | Go To

Find what: This is a hold-up, gimme the money

Check this to make sure Word looks for the same capitalisation you specify

5 Click to start the search

Less ↑ | Find Next | Cancel

Search Options

Search: All

☐ Match case
☐ Find whole words only
☐ Use wildcards
☐ Sounds like
☐ Find all word forms

Find

Format ▼ | Special ▼ | No Formatting

Specify special parameters for the search from this drop-down box

Search: All
Down
Up
All

4 Specify the controls

Specify whether the whole document is searched, or which direction the search takes, with this drop-down box

Special ▼

Paragraph Mark
Tab Character
Comment Mark
Any Character
Any Digit
Any Letter
Caret Character
Column Break
Em Dash
En Dash
Endnote Mark
Field
Footnote Mark
Graphic
Manual Line Break
Manual Page Break
Nonbreaking Hyphen
Nonbreaking Space
Optional Hyphen
Section Break
White Space

Format ▼
Font...
Paragraph...
Tabs...
Language...
Frame...
Style...
Highlight

Define the search formats from this drop-down box – selecting **Font**, say, leads you to the **Font** dialog box

Replacing

In the **Find and Replace** dialog box you may have noticed a tab marked **Replace**. Clicking this leads you to the **Replace** dialog box (or you can call up the dialog box directly). This lets you find text in the same way we've seen, then replaces the instances of text with a different text string. Say, your heroine's request for cash doesn't sound too cool, and you want to change it to something with a bit more class. Easy — get Word to replace it.

1 Choose **Edit ⇥ Replace**, or type ⎡Alt⎤+⎡E⎤ then ⎡E⎤, or type ⎡Ctrl⎤+⎡H⎤, or (as we've seen) click the **Replace** tab in the **Find** dialog box. This calls up the **Replace** dialog box

2 Enter the text string to look for

3 Type in the text string to replace it

4 Click the **More** button if you want to specify controls

5 Specify the controls (see page 91 for details)

6 Click the **Find Next** button to find the next occurrence of the string, or:

7 Begin the replacements using other buttons

Take note:

As you specify a format in either the Find dialog box or the Replace dialog box, the format is shown in the Format fields directly below the Find What and Replace With entry boxes (see opposite for example)

Tip:

While Word will happily find and replace text strings for you (formatted or unformatted) it is equally at home finding and replacing just formats (without any text string associated with them).

So, for example, you can find instances of text which are underlined (a fairly standard method of emphasising text) and replace them all with italicised text (*the usual typographers' emphasis method*) by specifying the formats to suit. Remember not to enter any text in either of the Find What or Replace With entry boxes

2 The text string to be found – leave blank if you're just looking for formats

1 **Replace** dialog box

4 Click for more controls

3 Text string to replace found text – leave blank if you're just wanting to replace formats

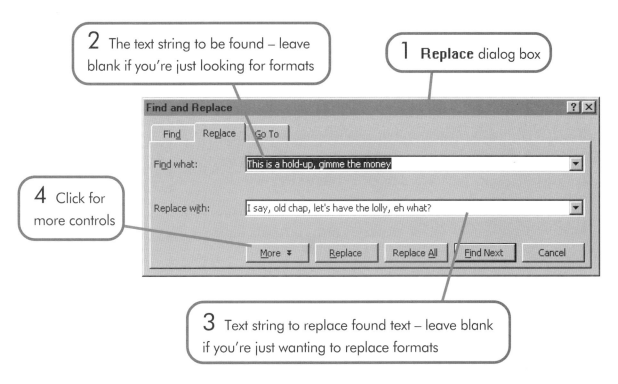

6 Click to find the next occurrence of the string

7 Click to replace the current occurrence of the string, and find the following occurrence
or: Click to replace all occurrences of the string

Click to clear formats from the active entry box

5 Specify the controls as shown on page 91

Spelling

One of Word's most useful tools is a spelling checker which looks through your document and compares each word with the words in an electronic dictionary. If Word finds a word in the dictionary, it assumes that word is spelled correctly.

Using Word's spelling checker you can rapidly check even the longest of documents — far more quickly than you could *read* through the document, at least.

Under default conditions the spelling checker works automatically, telling you of your spelling mistakes in two ways:

● highlighting the words it considers mis-spelled with a wavy red underline

● changing the spelling button on the status bar from its normal to — complete with a cross.

Making use of Word's spelling checker

Your course of action following notification of a spelling depends on

● whether you want to change the word at all (maybe it's a person's name, or a scientific word) which is actually spelled correctly but Word hasn't recognised it

● whether you want to add the word to Word's dictionary, so it won't be flagged up the next time you type it in

● whether you want to correct the spelling of a mis-spelled word

● whether you want to have the word corrected automatically by Word from now on.

IF THE WORD IS CORRECT

1 Click the underlined word with your right mouse button

2 Choose **Ignore All** from the drop-down menu — the underlined highlighting is removed from the word (and any other entries of the word)

Tip:

If you regularly type a word which Word assumes incorrectly is mis-spelled, add it to Word's dictionary. From the drop-down menu displayed opposite, choose Add. From now on, Word recognizses the word and ignores it

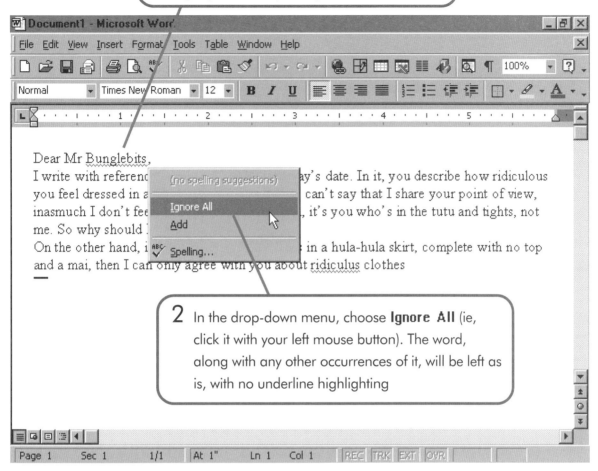

1 Click a correctly spelled word, that is underline highlighted, with your right mouse button

Dear Mr Bunglebits,
I write with referenc[e] ___ (no spelling suggestions) ___ ay's date. In it, you describe how ridiculous you feel dressed in a ___ can't say that I share your point of view, inasmuch I don't fee[l] — Ignore All ___, it's you who's in the tutu and tights, not me. So why should [I] — Add
On the other hand, i[f] — Spelling... in a hula-hula skirt, complete with no top and a mai, then I can only agree with you about ridiculus clothes

2 In the drop-down menu, choose **Ignore All** (ie, click it with your left mouse button). The word, along with any other occurrences of it, will be left as is, with no underline highlighting

Take note:

While Word's spelling checker is an extremely useful tool, you must remember that it only compares words in your document with the words in an electronic list called a dictionary. If the words in your document are mis-spelled in-context but in fact make properly spelled words out-of-context, Word *still* assumes they are spelled correctly. Thus, Word thinks *with complements* (instead of *with compliments*) is OK. Remember the anonymous ode:

> I have a spelling checker — it came with my pea see
> It plainly marques four my revue mistakes eye cannot sea
> I've run this poem threw it, I'm shore your pleased too no
> Its let a perfect inn it's weigh — my checquer told me sew

95

Spelling (contd)

Basic steps:

Tip:

You can have Word correct your bad spelling on-the-fly with AutoCorrect. If there's a word in particular you regularly misspell, click it with your right mouse button and choose Spelling from the drop-down menu. In the resultant dialog box type or choose the correct spelling and click AutoCorrect. From now on Word will correct it for you as you type it incorrectly

IF THE WORD IS INCORRECT

1 Click the underlined word with your right mouse button

2 Choose the correct spelling of the word from the drop-down menu

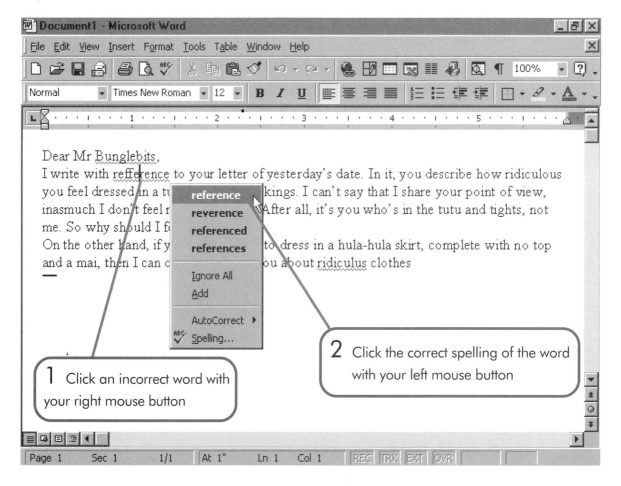

1 Click an incorrect word with your right mouse button

2 Click the correct spelling of the word with your left mouse button

1 Choose **Tools→Options** to call up the **Options** dialog box

2 Click the **Spelling and Grammar** tab

3 Change options to suit, then click **OK**

Word gives you several spelling options.

Tip:

If you get tired of the underline highlighting constantly reminding you of your bad spelling, turn it off by checking the Hide Spelling Errors in Current Document check box in the Spelling tab of the Options dialog box. The spelling button ▣ on the status bar still lets you know Word has found a spelling mistake, but it doesn't seem so persistent! Double-click the spelling button to jump to the next mis-spelled word

1 **Options** dialog box

2 **Spelling & Grammar** tab

Turn off/on Word's automatic spell checker

Turn off/on the annoying wavy red underline highlighting thingy

Turn off/on the annoying wavy green underline highlighting thingy

97

AutoCorrect

If you make the same spelling mistake regularly — say you always type *anf* instead of *and* (the author's problem; well, one of his problems, anyway) — Word's AutoCorrect feature is a boon.

To use AutoCorrect you simply have to specify which mistakes you make, and the correct spelling. Then whenever you make the mistake it is replaced automatically with the correct word.

Basic steps:

1 Call up the **AutoCorrect** dialog box by choosing **Tools ⯈ AutoCorrect**, or type ⌈Alt⌉+⌈T⌉ then ⌈A⌉

2 Type in the spelling mistake you often make into the **Replace** entry box, and the proper spelling in the **With** entry box

3 Click **Add** to add the word to the list

1 **AutoCorrect** dialog box

Check to turn AutoCorrect on – uncheck to turn it off

Other controls

2 Mistake you often make, and proper spelling

The AutoCorrect list – scroll through it to view, edit and delete entries

3 Click to add your entries to the AutoCorrect list

Click to accept

Tip:

Remember that you can create an AutoCorrect entry direct from the drop-down menu as you click an underline highlighted word with your right mouse button.

If you find that Word is finding the same spelling error repeatedly, follow the tip on page 96 to enter it automatically into the AutoCorrect list

Tip:

AutoCorrect can be used to insert chunks of text into a document when you type a simple keyword. For example, a phrase like *Yours sincerely,* at the end of a letter can have a keyword such as *ys*. As you type *ys* and hit the [Enter] or [↵] key, Word automatically replaces it with the longer phrase.

Phrases upto 255 characters (including spaces and punctuation) are possible, so a considerable amount of *boilerplate text* (as it's known in the computer business) can be accessed using AutoCorrect. For longer boilerplate text, and items you access less frequently, use Word's AutoText feature instead of AutoCorrect (see over)

Take note:

Word detects when you have finished a word — hence knows when to replace it, if it has an AutoCorrect entry — when an end-of-word specifier (usually a space) occurs.

So if the spelling error is followed by another letter, Word doesn't recognise the mistake and cannot correct it with AutoCorrect

Tip:

Not only text can be replaced by AutoCorrect entries. Graphics such as clip art can also be replaced; as can all formatting effects such as emboldening, sections, borders and shades.

Put your company letterhead into an AutoCorrect entry, and make light work of typing letters

AutoText

Word has the ability to greatly speed-up the entering of text you regularly use, in the guise of AutoText.

AutoCorrect, of course (see previous pages), allows you to do this as an automatic — on-the-fly as-you-type — feature. If you don't want it to occur automatically but instead want manual control over automatic insertion of entries, use AutoText.

To use an AutoText entry in your documents, you first have to create it.

CREATING AN ENTRY

1 Type the text, select it, then choose **Insert** �‣ **AutoText** ↣ **New**, or type Alt + F3 to call up the **AutoText** dialog box

2 Enter a new name for the entry (if the default name isn't suitable)

3 Click **OK** to accept the new entry

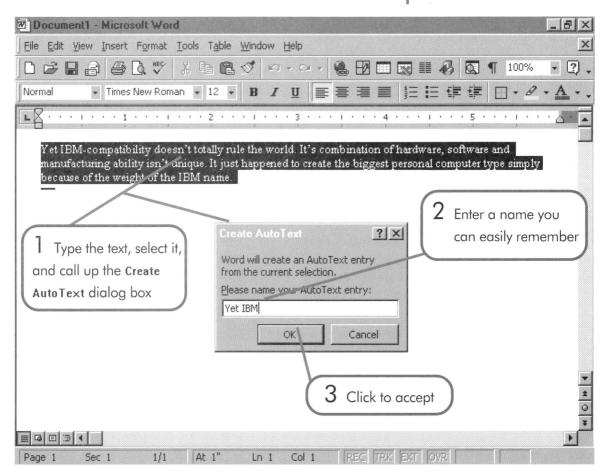

1 Type the text, select it, and call up the **Create AutoText** dialog box

2 Enter a name you can easily remember

3 Click to accept

1 When you want to insert an AutoText entry into your document, type in the entry name you previously allocated – as you do a ScreenTip is displayed which shows the first few words of the AutoText entry associated with the name

2 Hit Enter. The entry is inserted into the document

Once your entry is created, you can use it wherever and whenever you want in your documents.

> 1 When you want to insert an AutoText entry, simply type in the entry name…

I shall give you these with my complements. Take them home and keep them. Add other complimentary things to them to make them who Yet IBM-compatibility doesn't …
Yet IBM

ScreenTip shows you the AutoText entry associated with the name

I shall give you these with my complements. Take them home and keep them. Add other complimentary things to them to make them whole.
Yet IBM-compatibility doesn't totally rule the world. Its combination of hardware, software and manufacturing ability isn't unique. It just happened to create the biggest personal computer type simply because of the weight of the IBM name.

> 2 …then press Enter

Tip:

As with AutoCorrect, the entries you create for AutoText can include graphical items and text formatting. Like AutoCorrect entries, too, you can use AutoText to insert boilerplate text into your documents.

In fact, the only *real* difference between AutoText and AutoCorrect as far as ordinary users — you and me — are concerned, is how the entries are inserted into our documents:

❑ AutoCorrect entries are inserted automatically, as soon as the entry name is typed

❑ AutoText entries are inserted semi-automatically — *you* have to specify that the entry name be replaced with the entry.

They each have their uses

Outlining

We saw an outline view back on page 15. Outlining is another way of looking at your Word documents and, what's more important, is the best way of controlling how the various text parts within a document are organised and arranged.

Easiest way to see how outlining works is with an example. Let's say you've been working long and hard at a chapter of your book. It's a long chapter and technically quite involved — so involved that you're sure there's a problem somewhere, but you're not exactly sure *where*.

Basic steps:

1 Choose **View→Outline**, or type ⌈Alt⌉+⌈V⌉ then ⌈O⌉, or (best) click the Outline button 🔳 at the lower-left corner of the document window. Your document is displayed in outline view

1 A document in outline view

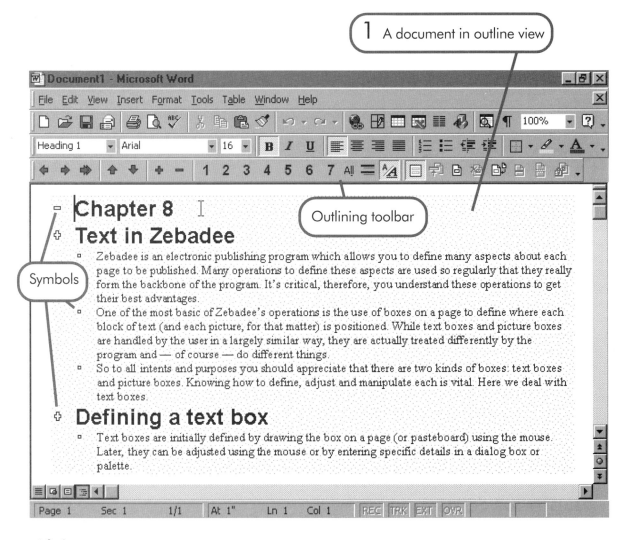

Outlining toolbar

Symbols

Chapter 8
Text in Zebadee

□ Zebadee is an electronic publishing program which allows you to define many aspects about each page to be published. Many operations to define these aspects are used so regularly that they really form the backbone of the program. It's critical, therefore, you understand these operations to get their best advantages.

□ One of the most basic of Zebadee's operations is the use of boxes on a page to define where each block of text (and each picture, for that matter) is positioned. While text boxes and picture boxes are handled by the user in a largely similar way, they are actually treated differently by the program and — of course — do different things.

□ So to all intents and purposes you should appreciate that there are two kinds of boxes: text boxes and picture boxes. Knowing how to define, adjust and manipulate each is vital. Here we deal with text boxes.

Defining a text box

□ Text boxes are initially defined by drawing the box on a page (or pasteboard) using the mouse. Later, they can be adjusted using the mouse or by entering specific details in a dialog box or palette.

Outline symbols

In outline view, your document is displayed with its headings and body text displayed with various symbols to their left. The symbols indicate what is associated with the various parts of a document.

Plus symbol indicates that a heading has either (or both) subheadings and body text beneath it

Minus symbol indicates that a heading has neither subheadings nor text beneath it

Box symbol indicates that text is body text (that is, it's not a heading of any kind)

Outlining toolbar

Along with outline view comes the Outlining toolbar, with its new buttons

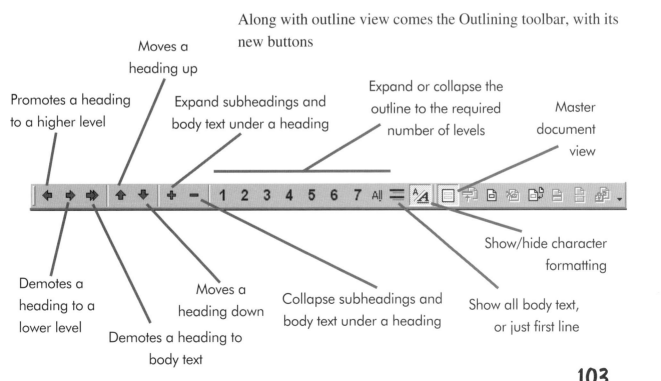

Promotes a heading to a higher level

Moves a heading up

Expand subheadings and body text under a heading

Expand or collapse the outline to the required number of levels

Master document view

Show/hide character formatting

Demotes a heading to a lower level

Moves a heading down

Demotes a heading to body text

Collapse subheadings and body text under a heading

Show all body text, or just first line

Outlining (contd)

In essence, outlining allows you to:

● get an overall view of your document — to various degrees of complexity

● easily move headings around (while their associated sub-headings and body text parts move automatically with them).

Another example can show you.

Document with character formatting
hidden and levels collapsed to level 1

Basic steps:

1 Click the Show/hide character formatting button [A̲] and the Expand/collapse to level 1 button [1] on the Outlining toolbar.

Now all character formatting has gone, and only the first level headings are displayed

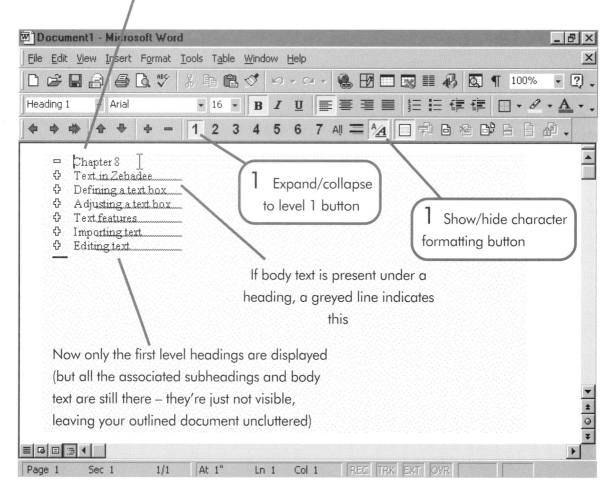

1 Expand/collapse to level 1 button

1 Show/hide character formatting button

If body text is present under a heading, a greyed line indicates this

Now only the first level headings are displayed (but all the associated subheadings and body text are still there – they're just not visible, leaving your outlined document uncluttered)

2 Select the headings Defining a text box, and Adjusting a text box. Now click the Demote heading button on the Outlining toolbar

3 Select the heading Editing text, then click the Move heading up button

From this position, let's now say you realise that:

● the level 1 headings *Defining a text box*, and *Adjusting a text box* really *should* be level 2 headings

● the heading *Editing text* should be before the heading *Importing text*.

With outlining, that's easily done.

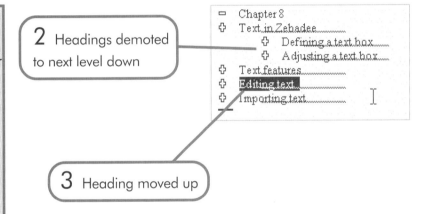

2 Headings demoted to next level down

3 Heading moved up

Tables

Earlier in the book we saw how to produce a simple table using tab stops. This is fine for just that — simple tables — but for anything more complex than just a couple of rows and columns things can be made much easier with Word's in-built table feature.

Tables are made up by a collection of *cells*, in rows and columns. Word displays a table in *gridlines* (dotted lines around all the cells of a table) which are not printed and are merely provided on-screen for guidance.

You can add text or graphical elements to cells of a Word table, and you can format text in any character or paragraph format as usual.

You create a table in one of two ways:

● from the **Insert Table** dialog box

● with the Table button on the Standard toolbar.

1 Position the insertion point where you want to create a table, then choose **Table⤳Insert⤳Table**, or type `Alt`+`A` then `I`, then `T`. This calls up the **Insert Table** dialog box

2 Enter the numbers of columns and rows you want

3 Click **OK** to create the table – Word displays the empty table as dotted gridlines

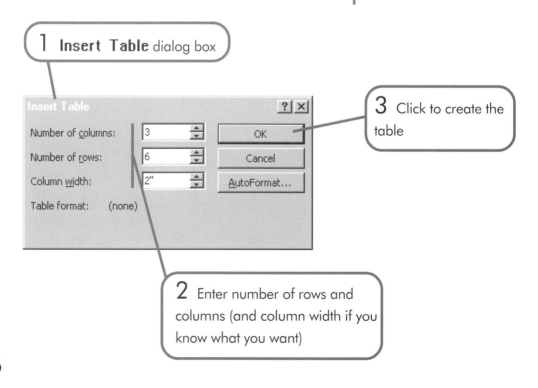

1 **Insert Table** dialog box

3 Click to create the table

2 Enter number of rows and columns (and column width if you know what you want)

106

1 Position the insertion point where you want to create a table, then click the Insert Table button 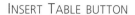 on the Standard toolbar

2 Drag across the drop-down grid to select the number of columns and rows you want, then let go the mouse button

1 Click to drop-down the table grid

2 Drag across grid to select the number of rows and columns you want

3 x 4 Table

The insertion point is positioned at the top-left cell in the table ready for you to enter text. You move around in a table by clicking the mouse in another cell, tabbing with the Tab key, or pressing the ↑↓←→ keys in the direction you want to move.

Press Tab to jump to next cell

Press Shift + Tab to jump to previous cell

Gridlines

Insertion point

Step through text within a cell using ↑↓←→ keys (once the insertion point reaches either end of text in a cell, further pressing of ↑↓←→ keys will jump to the next cell)

Tables (contd)

Once you've created a table you can change it to suit. You can drag column widths and indents from the document ruler (bottom) and you can drag a column gridline left or right to suit directly from the table.

Tip:

Whether you drag a column marker in the ruler or a table gridline, any more columns to the right of the moved element are resized proportionally — the table width doesn't change.

However, if you hold down Ctrl + Shift while you drag the table width *does* change

Ruler is active over active column

Text wraps around and row height increases if column width isn't sufficient

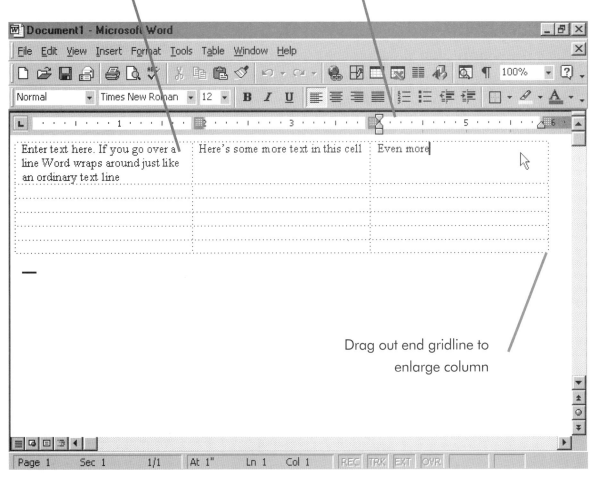

Drag out end gridline to enlarge column

Basic steps:

1 Select the text you want to convert to a table

2 Click the Insert Table button 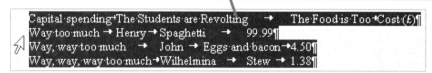 on the Standard toolbar – that text is converted into a table

Even if you've already entered text you can still convert it into a Word table. Simply make sure there are separators which Word recognises — commas or tabs between the items of text you want in each cell, and paragraph marks between each row — in the text.

1 Select the text you want to convert into a table – make sure it has adequate separators

Capital spending	The Students are Revolting	The Food is Too	Cost (£)
Way too much	Henry	Spaghetti	99.99
Way, way too much	John	Eggs and bacon	4.50
Way, way, way too much	Wilhelmina	Stew	1.38

Capital spending¤	The Students are Revolting¤	The Food is Too¤	Cost (£)¤
Way too much¤	Henry¤	Spaghetti¤	99.99¤
Way, way too much¤	John¤	Eggs and bacon¤	4.50¤
Way, way, way too much¤	Wilhelmina¤	Stew¤	1.38¤

2 Converted into a table

Tip:

Cells can easily be merged together — useful, for example, if you want to have a heading over a number of columns. Just select the cells you want to merge, then choose Table↦Merge Cells, or type Alt + A, then M

Take note:

You can convert a table into text, too, in a similar way. First select the rows you want to convert into text then choose Table↦Convert Table to Text. Then, in the Convert Table to Text dialog box, choose the character you want to separate table cell text with, and click OK

Convert Table To Text

Separate text with
- ○ Paragraph marks
- ● Tabs
- ○ Commas
- ○ Other: [-]

[OK] [Cancel]

Table formatting

Once you've created a table, you can format it in all the usual ways. However, Word gives you several suggested options to format it automatically, which are both faster and (probably) better than doing it manually.

1 Select the table and choose **Table⇥Table AutoFormat**, or type ⟨Alt⟩+⟨A⟩ then ⟨F⟩, to call up the **Table AutoFormat** dialog box

2 From the list of formats select one you want

3 Click **OK** to accept this format onto your table

1 **Table AutoFormat** dialog box

2 Scroll through list to select a table format

Preview gives an example of format

3 Click to accept your selected format

Other controls over formatting

The table on the previous page, formatted with the Classic 4 format above

Counting your words

Basic steps:

1 Choose **Tools⤷Word Count**, or type Alt + T then W, to call up the **Word Count** dialog box

When all your text has been entered into a document, it's often necessary to count the total number of words in it. Most publishers need a word count, for example, to give some idea of how long a document is, therefore a rough estimate of how many pages it'll fill in the finished publication.

Word can do much more than just count the words in a document, however.

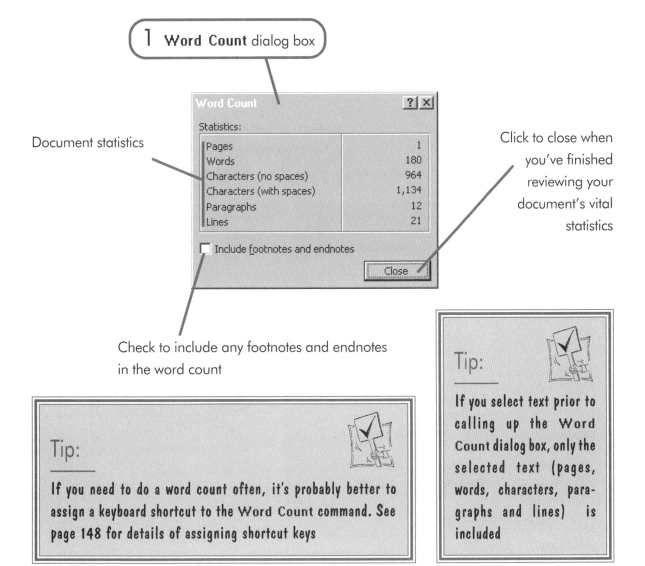

1 **Word Count** dialog box

Document statistics

Word Count

Statistics:

Pages	1
Words	180
Characters (no spaces)	964
Characters (with spaces)	1,134
Paragraphs	12
Lines	21

☐ Include footnotes and endnotes

Close

Click to close when you've finished reviewing your document's vital statistics

Check to include any footnotes and endnotes in the word count

Tip:

If you need to do a word count often, it's probably better to assign a keyboard shortcut to the Word Count command. See page 148 for details of assigning shortcut keys

Tip:

If you select text prior to calling up the Word Count dialog box, only the selected text (pages, words, characters, paragraphs and lines) is included

Graphics

You can import a graphic created in another application into a Word document. There are several kinds of graphic files you may want to import, but the principle is the same, whatever the kind. Also, once imported, any graphic can be edited in several ways.

Basic steps:

IMPORTING A GRAPHIC

1 Position the insertion point where you want the graphic to be placed. Choose **Insert� ⃗Picture ↳From File**, or type `Alt`+`I` then `P`, then `F`

2 Locate the graphic you want in the **Insert Picture** dialog box and click **OK**. The graphic is imported to your document

2 Locate graphic file you want to import

1 **Insert Picture** dialog box

Click this button, and choose Preview from the drop-down menu to preview picture in box below

Resizing a graphic

RESIZING A GRAPHIC

1 Click a graphic in a Word document

2 Drag any of the box handles to adjust the size or shape

Once a graphic file has been imported into a Word document, editing is simple — the most basic form of editing (and the one most commonly undertaken) is resizing to suit the document.

1 Select a graphic by clicking it

As you let go the mouse button, the graphic resizes itself

2 Drag a box handle to resize a graphic. Dragging a corner handle resizes the graphic proportionally. Dragging a middle handle resizes it disproportionately

Take note:

Word uses special files called graphics filters to let it import graphics files. While Windows bitmaps (with the extension *.bmp*). Windows metafiles (*.wmf*) and tag image file format files (*.tif*) are imported directly, you need filters (available from Microsoft) to import other graphics file formats

Editing graphics

You can make use of the Picture toolbar in Word to edit graphics you have imported into a document. The basis of its operation is that you have to select a graphic (by clicking it) then choose the operation you want to perform from the toolbar buttons.

Tip:

You can use the Picture toolbar to insert a graphic in the first place — so if you use a lot of graphics it's worth leaving the Picture toolbar handy

Basic steps:

You can call up the Picture toolbar in one of two main ways:

1 Right-click any toolbar and check the Picture toolbar check box (as on page 8)

or:

2 Choose
View ↳ Toolbars ↳ Picture

2 Choose
View ↳ Toolbars ↳ Picture

1 Right-click, then choose **Picture**

The Picture toolbar controls the active (that is, the selected graphic)

Picture toolbar buttons

The buttons on the Picture toolbar are shown below:

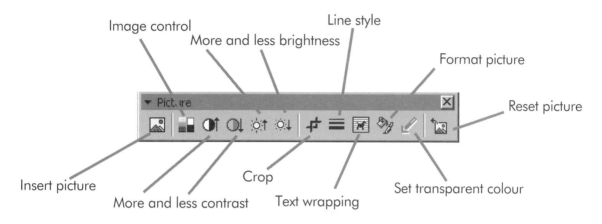

Picture formatting

An alternative to working with the Picture toolbar is to use the
Format Picture dialog box. Double-click a graphic to call up
this dialog box.

Clip art

On install, Word has many graphics files included — called clip art — that you can make use of, in the same way that you use your purpose-created graphics files.

> ## Tip:
>
> **Look on your original CD-ROM installer for Word — there are many more clip art files on it**

1 **Insert ClipArt** dialog box

Basic steps:

1 Position the insertion point where you want the graphic to be placed. Choose **Insert↳ Picture↳Clip Art**, or type `Alt`+`I` then `P`, then `C`

2 Clip art is arranged in categories. Scroll through the category list to located the category you want, then click its icon

2 Click the category corresponding to the sort of clip art you want

3 Locate the clip art you want and click it

4 In the drop-down menu, choose what you want to do with the clip art

3 Click the clip art you want – note the pop-up information

4 Choose your option from the drop-down menu – see below

 Insert clip art – clicking this button imports the clip art into your Word document

 Add clip to Favorites or other category – lets you file the clip art into another category

 Preview clip – displays the clip art as a larger preview

 Find similar clips – continues search for other clip art

Summary

❑ Use Word's powerful find and replace commands to search for and change text or even just formatting within your documents.

❑ Word's spelling checker can locate instances of mis-spelled words, but remember that a word mis-spelt in-context may still make a word spelled correctly out-of-context.

❑ Use AutoCorrect to correct spelling mistakes you regularly make, and automatically insert phrases at your abbreviated prompt.

❑ Use AutoText to insert phrases at your manual prompt.

❑ Remember that outlining helps you to organise your documents logically, and can be a boon when writing too.

❑ Tables in Word can be most effectively created with the **Table** command.

❑ Use Word's useful **Word Count** command to keep a check on how many words long your document is.

❑ You can import certain graphics files into your Word documents, then edit them in various ways.

6 Automatic formatting

Styles

Styles are the first method of automatic formatting. They are *extremely* important, because:

● their use makes it easy to define the formats which any particular paragraph has applied to it

● styles are groups of formats gathered together under one label (all the formats considered in Chapter 3 — and some others — can be gathered together and given just a single style name)

● if you apply a style to selected text *all* that text has the same formats applied to it simultaneously

● all you need to do to apply a style to selected text is choose that style from a drop-down list — the text is formatted with all the individual formats just by this one action

● you can use styles instantly, because any Word document has default styles already built in.

1 Enter some text into a new Word document. Don't bother applying any character or paragraph formats yet. Make sure you type in a few para-graphs and make the top paragraph and some others single line ones – say headings or subhead-ings

2 Select the top heading of the document (you can simply click anywhere in the first paragraph) then click the Style drop-down list box of the Formatting toolbar

Report into the oxidation of ferrous materials under load conditions
Oxidation defined
Under most circumstances, ferrous materials have iron in them. Iron is a substance wh
combines with oxygen under certain conditions, forming a chemical compound called
oxide.
Oxides are often of no concern — aluminum oxide for example is actually of some
benefit in aluminum substances because it creates a hard barrier against physical dama
to the rest of the material.
Ferrous oxide, on the other hand, *is* of concern. Ferrous oxide, aka iron oxide, aka rust is
of particular importance because:
it is unsightly
it is weaker than its non-oxidised counterpart.
Load conditions
Under certain conditions ferrous oxidation occurs more rapidly than under other
conditions. There are two critical conditions which, when applied together to ferrous
materials, make the likelihood of oxidation much greater. These two conditions are:
application of moisture in the form of water or water vapour
application of oxygen in the form of gas.
It is reasonably safe to say that if either of these conditions can be prevented then ferrous
oxidation does not occur.

2 Select the top paragraph of the entered text – you don't need to select the whole paragraph, you only need to click in it

1 Enter unformatted text into your document

3 From the Style drop-down list (a list of the default styles present in each new Word document) choose Heading 1

4 View the results of this style change

3 The Style drop-down list box. Default styles for Word documents are listed

4 The style applied to the top paragraph – the document's heading

Note how the whole paragraph has been formatted with the formats contained within the Heading 1 style

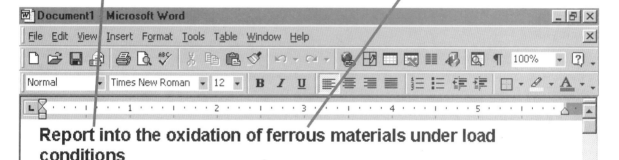

Report into the oxidation of ferrous materials under load conditions

Oxidation defined

Under most circumstances, ferrous materials have iron in them. Iron is a substance which combines with oxygen under certain conditions, forming a chemical compound called an oxide.

Oxides are often of no concern — aluminum oxide for example is actually of some benefit in aluminum substances because it creates a hard barrier against physical damage to the rest of the material.

Ferrous oxide, on the other hand, *is* of concern. Ferrous oxide, aka iron oxide, aka rust is of particular importance because:

it is unsightly

it is weaker than its non-oxidised counterpart.

Load conditions

Under certain conditions ferrous oxidation occurs more rapidly than under other conditions. There are two critical conditions which, when applied together to ferrous

Styles (contd)

5 Continue applying styles
in the same way, trying
out the other heading
styles available

5 Apply other styles to your document in the same way as before

Heading 1   Heading 2

Document1 - Microsoft Word

File Edit View Insert Format Tools Table Window Help

Normal ▾ Times New Roman ▾ 12 ▾ **B** *I* U ≡ ≡ ≡ ≡ ⋮≡ ⋮≡ 律 律 □ ▾ ✎ ▾ **A** ▾ ▾

Report into the oxidation of ferrous materials under load conditions

Oxidation defined

Under most circumstances, ferrous materials have iron in them. Iron is a substance which combines with oxygen under certain conditions, forming a chemical compound called an oxide.

Oxides are often of no concern — aluminum oxide for example is actually of some benefit in aluminum substances because it creates a hard barrier against physical damage to the rest of the material.

Ferrous oxide, on the other hand, *is* of concern. Ferrous oxide, aka iron oxide, aka rust is of particular importance because:

it is unsightly

it is weaker than its non-oxidised counterpart.

Load conditions

Page 1   Sec 1   1/1   At 1"   Ln 1   Col 1   REC TRK EXT OVR

Heading 3

Character and paragraph styles

There are two types of styles:

● character styles

● paragraph styles.

They are identified by their appearance in the Styles drop-down list of the Formatting toolbar. They work in essentially the same way (that is, you select the text to be stylised, then select the style) but what they do to the selected text differs.

Paragraph styles are displayed with a paragraph symbol after them. When you apply a paragraph font to selected text, the whole paragraph has the formats applied

Character styles are displayed with a character symbol after them. When you apply a character style to text, only selected text (that is, not the whole paragraph – unless the whole paragraph is selected!) has the formats applied

Take note:

Styles are important for at least two reasons:

● because they speed up the way you can format a document. Rather than formatting each selection of text with individual character and paragraph formats (which can take some time if you have quite a few formats to apply) you can apply *all* the formats in one operation

● because the formats you apply as a style are always the same, there is no chance that you have forgotten any particular formats — if you apply each format individually you will probably forget some of them — all text with a particular style applied is identical in formats

Creating styles

There are three main ways you can create your own paragraph style:

● apply formats to your own sample text, until it is the way you want it, then create the style from those formats (for most people, this is ideal)

● adapt another style to suit

● copy styles from other documents to your own.

1 To create a style from your own sample text, apply formats to your text until it is the way you want it (look again at Chapter 3 if you're a bit hazy about formatting)

2 Select the text you want to make a style of

1 Apply different formats to text until it is as you want

2 Select formatted text to make a style

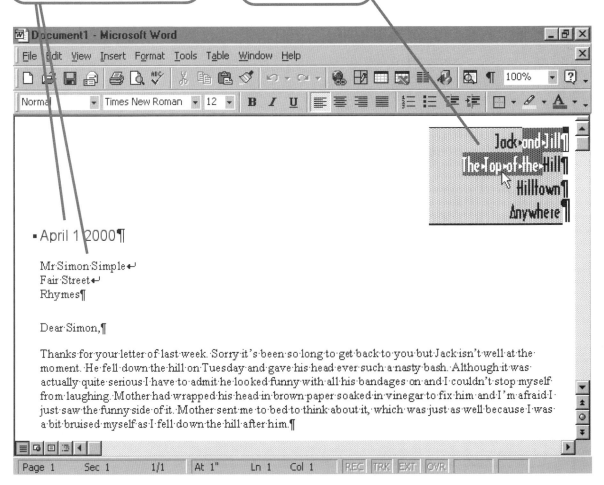

3 Choose **Format ↪ Style**, or type ⌨ Alt + ⌨ O then ⌨ S, to call up the **Style** dialog box. Click **New** to call up the **New Style** dialog box

4 Enter a name for the style

5 Check the **Add to Template** check box, then click **OK**, then click **Close** in the **Style** dialog box

If you repeat this procedure for all the different styles within your document, when you have finished you will end up with a number of styles which have been added to Word (in the Normal template, actually), and which will be present whenever you open a new document following that template.

Next time you want to produce a similar looking document the styles are already there to use. Simply enter your text in the new document, select the text to be formatted with any particular style, then apply the style from the Formatting toolbar's Style button drop-down list. The text is formatted as you defined.

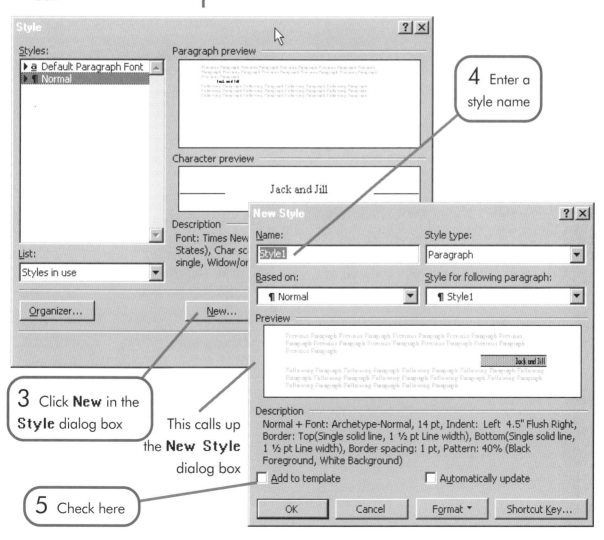

4 Enter a style name

3 Click **New** in the **Style** dialog box

This calls up the **New Style** dialog box

5 Check here

Creating styles (contd)

One of the beauties of styles is their ability to be modified. What's more, if you modify a style *all* text in a document which has been formatted with that style is modified too. This is extremely useful when you're formatting a document to appear how you want it, but also it's a useful method of creating your own styles.

MODIFY EXISTING STYLE

1 Choose **Format⇥Style**, or type [Alt]+[O] then [S]

2 In the **Style** dialog box, select the style you want to modify in the **Styles** entry list, then click **Modify** to call up the **Modify** dialog box

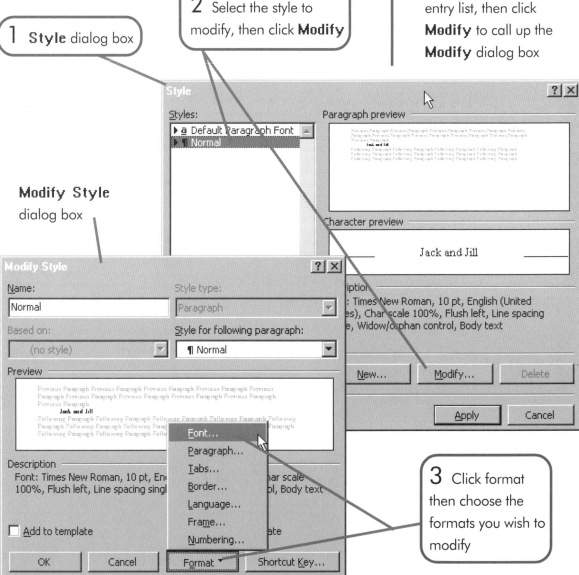

1 Style dialog box

2 Select the style to modify, then click **Modify**

Modify Style dialog box

3 Click format then choose the formats you wish to modify

126

3 Click the **Format** button
to drop-down a list of
modifiable formats, select
the format you want and
in the resultant dialog box
adjust formats to suit.
Repeat this if you want to
modify more than one
format type

Take note:

When you click the Format button at step 3, you can modify any
of the formats we've seen already (along with some new ones).
All the formats available in the drop-down list are assigned to
the style — then, when you have finished, all text which is
formatted with that style is modified too. In other words, you
can make some immense changes to the appearance of your
document quite simply just by modifying a style

Tip:

You can assign keyboard shortcuts to any style — simply modify the style as suggested here, and
in the Modify Style dialog box click Shortcut Key, to call up the Customize dialog box with
its Keyboard tab active. Enter the shortcut you want assigned to the style and if that shortcut isn't already used for some other function click Assign. Click Close, then OK in the Modify Style dialog box, followed by Close in the Style dialog box.

Now you can apply a style simply by selecting the text and pressing your keyboard shortcut

Creating styles (contd)

The last method of creating styles in a document is to copy styles from other documents which have the styles you want. It's the **Organizer** dialog box which allows you to do this, listing styles in two documents side-by-side, so that you can copy styles from one to the other.

The styles to be copied can be in a true Word document, or in a Word template. Word has many default templates which you can use for this purpose, and we'll use one to illustrate how you can do it.

Basic steps:

COPYING STYLES

1 To copy one or more styles from one document to another, choose **Format↦Style**, or type ⌐Alt⌐+⌐O⌐ then ⌐S⌐, to call up the **Style** dialog box. Click the **Organizer**

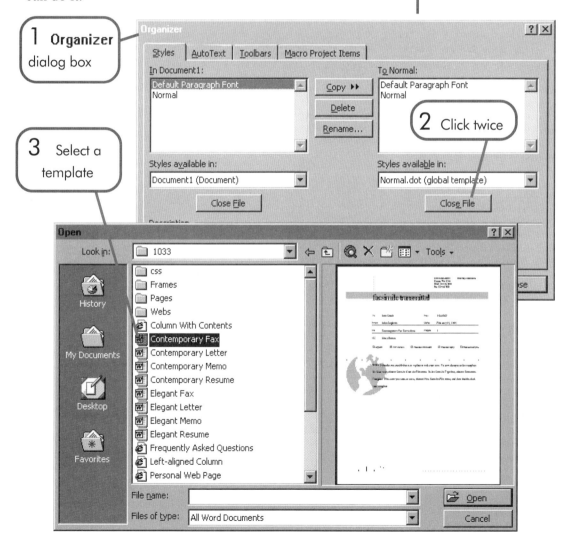

1 **Organizer** dialog box

2 Click twice

3 Select a template

button to call up the **Organizer** dialog box

2 Click **Close File** on the right side of the dialog box (the button changes to **Open File**) then click **Open File**. This displays a list of available files you can select. Locate the templates directory in the MSOffice directory on your hard disk if neces-

sary, using the **Open** dialog box

3 Select a template in the list and click **Open**. Now the **Organizer** dialog box displays all the styles in the template in a scrollable list

4 You can select individual styles, or you can select

multiple styles by 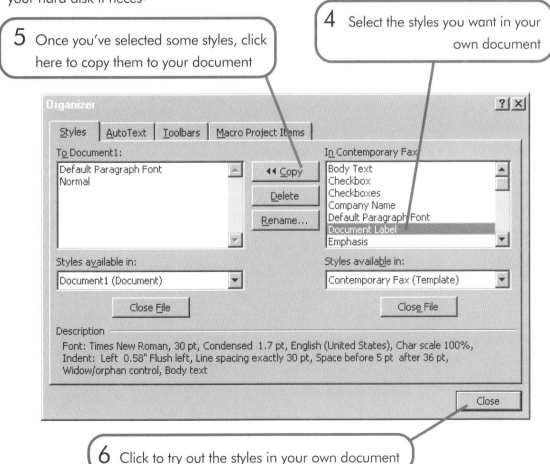Ctrl + clicking them

5 Copy them to your own document by clicking **Copy**

6 Click **Close** to close the **Organizer** dialog box, then try out your new styles in your own document

5 Once you've selected some styles, click here to copy them to your document

4 Select the styles you want in your own document

Organizer   ?|X|

| Styles | AutoText | Toolbars | Macro Project Items |

To Document1:

Default Paragraph Font
Normal

◄◄ Copy

Delete

Rename...

In Contemporary Fax:

Body Text
Checkbox
Checkboxes
Company Name
Default Paragraph Font
Document Label
Emphasis

Styles available in:

Document1 (Document)

Styles available in:

Contemporary Fax (Template)

Close File   Close File

Description

Font: Times New Roman, 30 pt, Condensed 1.7 pt, English (United States), Char scale 100%, Indent: Left 0.58" Flush left, Line spacing exactly 30 pt, Space before 5 pt after 36 pt, Widow/orphan control, Body text

Close

6 Click to try out the styles in your own document

More about styles

If you haven't already realised it, styles are very important to a word processor like Word. Styles form the key to producing professional documents with total consistency of formatting. Their use ensures efficient control over your documents.

However, there's a few additional things to know about styles which can make their use even more efficient. They are presented here as a collection of tips and notes — bear them in mind when you use Word.

Tip:

When you create a new document, base it on a template — templates are complete with their own styles which you can use immediately. If there's a particular style of document you want, design it then save it as a template. Each time you create a new document based on that template it'll be exactly as you want it (see page 134)

Tip:

Format all text in a document with styles — that way if you want to change the document's appearance you only have to change a handful of styles, not the various text elements

Tip:

While we've said all along how you should enter all your text first, then apply styles to it there is a more elegant way which calls on Word styles' ability to change to another style when a paragraph ends. In either the New Style or the Modify Style dialog boxes there is a drop-down list box called Style for Following Paragraph. In here is a list of all available styles. Choose one. Then as your style which has a specified style to follow ends, the next style comes into force.

This is useful, say, for headings and subheadings (which are nearly always of a single paragraph and are followed by, say, normal style). As you finish typing the heading text and press ⏎ or Enter, the next paragraph is automatically stylised with the next style

130

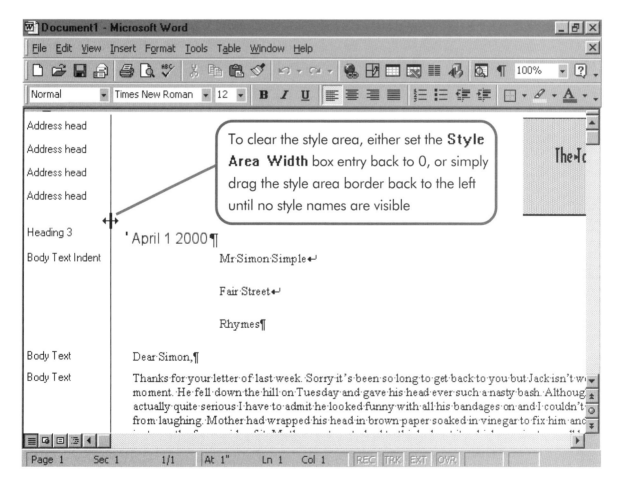

To clear the style area, either set the **Style Area Width** box entry back to 0, or simply drag the style area border back to the left until no style names are visible

More about styles (contd)

Check this to make sure a heading stays with its following text, without being left at the bottom of a page

Check this to create a page break before a major heading – in other words the major heading will always start at the top of a page

Styles are probably the most important feature of a word processor like Word. If you manage the styles in your documents properly, taking care in how they are formatted, how they are based, what text flow is associated with them and so on, your documents will be much better for it. Not only do they look *better*, but it is also much easier to make large formatting changes to suit the way you want your documents to look. For example, if all styles are based properly on each other in a hierarchical way a single change of font or size will change the whole document

If you change a font, or any other formatting parameter, in a style which another style is based on, the other style's font (or other parameter) changes too — unless you have already specified a different parameter in the second style

You can use the above to advantage when you set up the styles in your document — to specify the style which will follow another style. For example, if you specify that a heading is followed by body text then, every time you type a heading and press Enter or ⏎ (as long as Word knows that the heading *is* a heading — see next paragraph), the next paragraph will be in the body text style.

To enter styles as you go along, you *can* select the style from the style list box in the Formatting toolbar, but it's a lot easier to assign the style a keyboard shortcut which you can enter whenever you want to change style

If you can't be bothered to arrange styles to best suit your documents, at least use Word's AutoFormat command. This does a largely similar job, automatically — properly defines styles are always better, on the other hand

About templates

In places throughout the book, the term *template* has been used, without any clear explanation. Now it's time to say exactly *what* a template is.

Effectively, a template is a skeleton document. It has all the bones of any document, in terms of document parameters — just not all the flesh in terms of text you enter.

Word uses templates to store all document parameters. Character and paragraph formats, tables, styles, sections, AutoText entries, graphical items and so on — and even text — can all be stored in a template.

Then, when you create a new document, you can base it on the chosen template and up pops a new document looking exactly as you want it — all you need to do is enter any final details and *hey, presto!*, a complete document. You could use a template, for example, when you create a letter. In the template might be a letterhead, complete with a company logo, and styles which specify fonts and formats for use in the letter. Another example could be a template setup for your monthly sales figures — the document is complete; you just add the figures. See over for details of creating your own template.

A default installation of Word includes a number of built-in templates as standard. When you first start up Word, the first document on-screen is even based on a template (the Normal template, actually). When you create a *new* document, on the other hand, you are given an option to choose which of the built-in templates you want to use for the document.

Basic steps:

1 Choose **File→New**, or type [Alt]+[F] then [N], or type [Ctrl]+[N]. This calls up the **New** dialog box

2 Click a tab to see the templates that are associated with it

3 Click a template

4 Click **Template** if you want to create a new template based on the template chosen

5 Click **OK** to create the document based on that template

Tip:

You can bypass the New dialog box if you merely want to create a document speedily. Just click the New button [ ] on the Standard toolbar and a new document — based on the Normal template — is automatically created

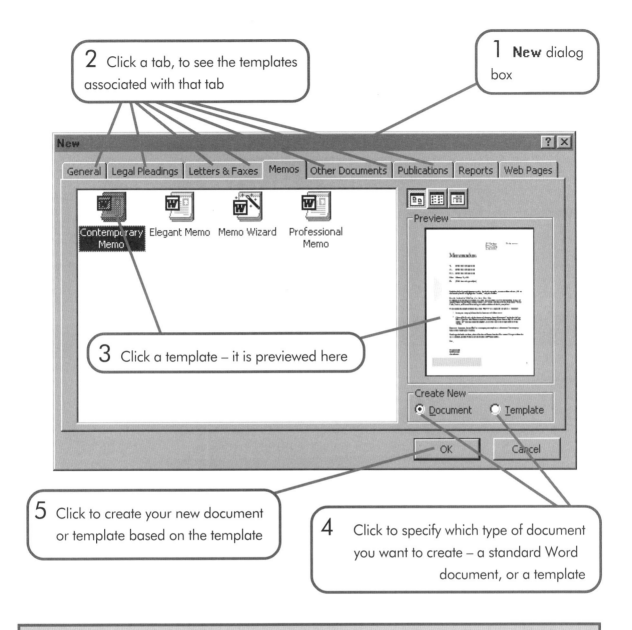

2 Click a tab, to see the templates associated with that tab

1 **New** dialog box

3 Click a template – it is previewed here

5 Click to create your new document or template based on the template

4 Click to specify which type of document you want to create – a standard Word document, or a template

Take note:

The Normal template is a special case template — it holds all the document parameters you use most in Word. All the toolbars, their buttons, their positions, the menus and shortcut keys, and everything else you have as default items, are stored in the Normal template. If you use another template to create other documents, on the other hand, all these features are still available

Creating a template

It's easy to create your own template. If there's a document type you find you're using quite a lot, it's worth making a template of it, then whenever you want to create another document with the same style just create the document from the template.

Once you've got the document looking just the way you want it (remember, you only need the bare bones of it), follow the steps here.

Basic steps:

1 Choose **File ⤳ Save As**, or type **Alt** + **F** then **A**. This calls up the **Save As** dialog box

2 Click the **Save File as Type** drop-down list box to see the drop-down list of types you can save the document as

3 Select **Document Template**

4 Enter a name for your template

5 Click **Save**

> 1 **Save As** dialog box

> 4 Enter a name you'll remember

> 5 Click to save template

> 2 Click to drop-down the drop-down menu

> 3 Select the **Document Template** option

136

Here's an example of a template for a letterhead. It combines a heading with a border (the underlining) and a simple graphic

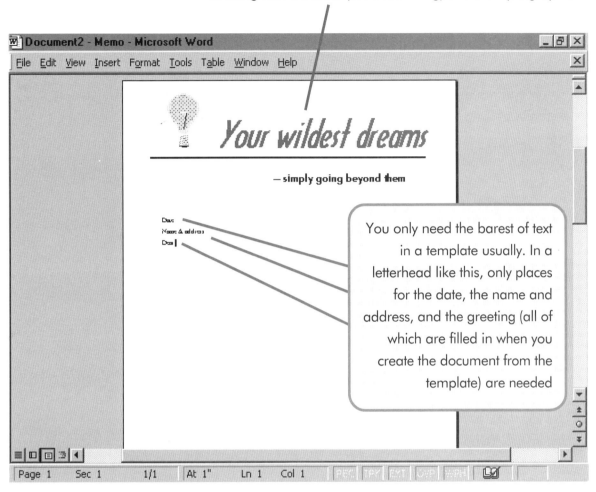

Your wildest dreams

— simply going beyond them

You only need the barest of text in a template usually. In a letterhead like this, only places for the date, the name and address, and the greeting (all of which are filled in when you create the document from the template) are needed

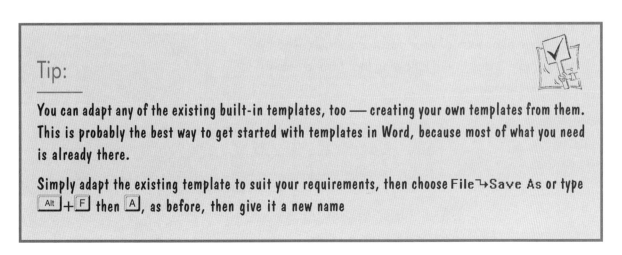

Tip:

You can adapt any of the existing built-in templates, too — creating your own templates from them. This is probably the best way to get started with templates in Word, because most of what you need is already there.

Simply adapt the existing template to suit your requirements, then choose File↪Save As or type Alt+F then A, as before, then give it a new name

Summary

❑ Use styles containing all formatting parameters you need in a document.

❑ Set up styles which are based on other styles. Use a hierarchy of styles to create your document.

❑ There are two kinds of styles – paragraph and character styles.

❑ To create styles (1) apply formats to a sample of text then create the style from those formats, (2) adapt an existing style, or (3) copy styles from other documents (or templates).

❑ Use keyboard shortcuts to help you apply styles.

❑ Make sure headings (1) stay with the following paragraph – to prevent a heading being left at the bottom of the page – and (2) have a following style – to make sure your body style, say, is automatically applied when you press Enter or ⏎. Use styles to do this.

❑ Use templates to speed up how you create good-looking documents. Templates hold skeleton information about a document – styles, graphics, some text – you only need to fill in the meat on the bones.

❑ If you find yourself using the same type of document over and over again, set up a template comprising the fundamental aspects of your document. Then, when you go to create a document following that type, create it from your template.

7 Technical thingamajigs

Print preview

Before you print a document, it's best to stand back and take a look at it. Print previewing does this job for you, giving you an overall view of the document before you go ahead and waste your paper while letting you edit the document if you need.

Print preview brings with it its own toolbar, with some new buttons.

Basic steps:

1 Choose **File ↳Print Preview**, or type `Alt`+`F` then `V`, or simply (best) click the Print Preview button 🔍 on the Standard toolbar. The display changes to print preview, fitting complete pages of your document into the print preview window

2 Use buttons on the Print Preview toolbar to adjust the display to suit

2 Print preview toolbar

Click to print

Zoom entry box and drop-down list

Display rulers

Shrink to Fit – if there's only a small amount of text on the document's last page, clicking here might (if you're lucky) take the text back to fit on one page less

33%   Close ▶?

Magnifier (active on screen opposite)

Display multiple pages (two shown opposite)

Full-screen view

Display a single page

140

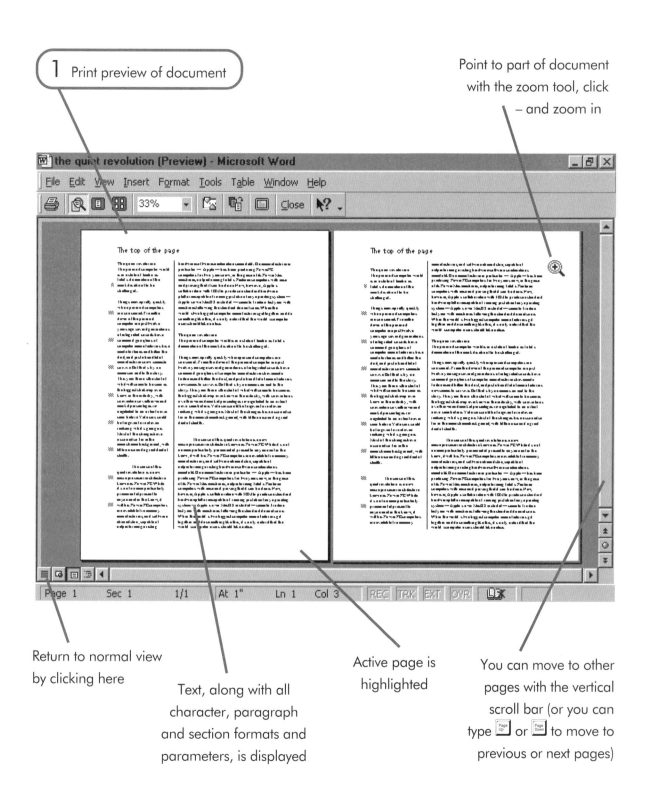

1 Print preview of document

Point to part of document with the zoom tool, click – and zoom in

Return to normal view by clicking here

Text, along with all character, paragraph and section formats and parameters, is displayed

Active page is highlighted

You can move to other pages with the vertical scroll bar (or you can type Page Up or Page Down to move to previous or next pages)

Printing

While printing from a PC can give many headaches, use of the Windows environment coupled with Word itself makes life a lot easier. We have, however, to assume that your computer is properly connected to a printer, and that both are on and working. After that, there are only a few things you need to know.

Basic steps:

1 Choose **File↵Print**, or type [Alt]+[F] then [P], or type [Ctrl]+[P]. This calls up the **Print** dialog box

2 As the default dialog box stands, if you click **OK**, one copy of the text in the active document will be printed to the printer shown – you can adjust controls and entries to change this

The printer currently selected

Specify which pages you want to print

Click to view and change various printing options (see opposite)

(1 **Print** dialog box)

How many copies do you want?

(2 Click to print)

Drop-down list to specify which part of the document you want to print

Drop-down list allows you to print both sides, or specified sides of double-sided documents

Printing options

1 Follow step 1 (left), then click **Options**. This calls up the **Printing options** dialog box

Apart from controlling print parameters such as number of copies, which pages and so on, you can specify other, more technical, things too. Important ones are shown below.

Tip:

You can speed up the printing process by simply clicking the Print button 🖨 on the Standard toolbar. This bypasses the Print dialog box altogether and prints the document with default settings — for most printing purposes this is fine

1 Call up the **Printing options** dialog box

Uses draft mode of printer to print rapid copies. Not all features of your documents may be printed

Prints in background (allowing you to get on with your work while printing takes place)

Prints pages of your documents in reverse order

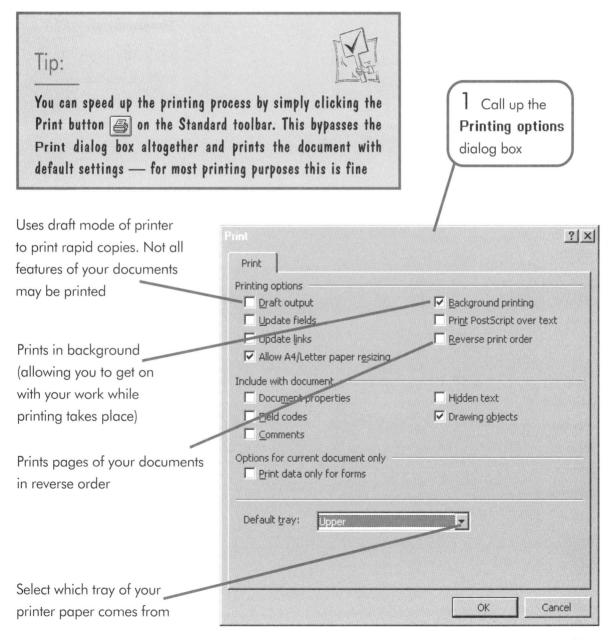

Select which tray of your printer paper comes from

Starting Word at turn-on

If you use Word just about every time you turn on your computer, you can set it up to start Word (or any other program for that matter) automatically.

1 Choose **🔳Start** ↳ **Settings** ↳ **Taskbar**, this calls up the **Taskbar Properties** dialog box

2 Click the **Start Menu Programs** tab

3 Click **Advanced**. This calls up an Explorer window, for the Start Menu

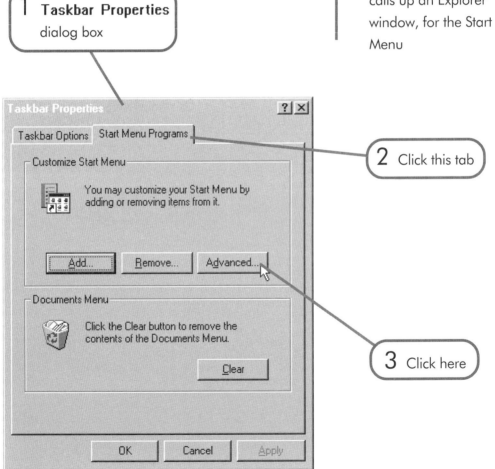

1 **Taskbar Properties** dialog box

Taskbar Properties

Taskbar Options | Start Menu Programs

Customize Start Menu

You may customize your Start Menu by adding or removing items from it.

Add... | Remove... | Advanced...

2 Click this tab

Documents Menu

Click the Clear button to remove the contents of the Documents Menu.

Clear

3 Click here

OK | Cancel | Apply

4 Click the + box, to open the **Programs** folder in the left half of the window. If Microsoft Word is in this folder, go to step 5. If MSOffice is in the **Programs** folder, open the **MSOffice** folder in the same way

5 Hold down `Ctrl` and drag the Microsoft Word icon from the right half of the window to the **StartUp** folder in the left half

Tip:

Holding down `Ctrl` while dragging *copies* the Word icon to the StartUp folder. Dragging without holding `Ctrl` would merely move it! Now, whenever you restart your computer Word will automatically startup. If you ever want this *not* to happen, simply delete the icon

4 Open the **Programs** folder – you may need to open the **MSOffice** folder too, depending on how Word is installed on your computer

5 Hold down `Ctrl` and drag the Microsoft Word icon to the **StartUp** folder in the **Programs** folder

Toolbars

While Word has a large number of toolbars, they may not always be to a user's liking. Either they might have the wrong buttons on for your particular tasks, or they might not have the buttons you want at all.

You can customize toolbars (by adding, deleting, changing and moving around buttons), and you can create your own toolbars (designing buttons from scratch if you want). You can also choose from a wide range of built-in buttons to assign to commands in Word.

Basic steps:

ADAPTING A TOOLBAR

1 Choose **Tools** ↪ **Customize**, or type `Alt` + `T` then `C`, to call up the **Customize** dialog box

2 Click the **Commands** tab if it's not already frontmost

3 Drag a button onto the toolbar of your choice to add it (or drag a button off a toolbar to delete it)

2 Click **Commands** if not already frontmost

1 **Customize** dialog box

Built-in buttons available for commands in the chosen category

3 Drag the chosen button to the toolbar of your choice

Categories of commands

Save changes to a template (default is Normal.dot – which means changes affect all your Word documents)

146

CREATING A TOOLBAR

1 In the **Customize** dialog box, click the **Toolbars** tab

2 Click **New**, to call up the **New Toolbar** dialog box

3 Give the new toolbar a name

4 Click **OK** – the new toolbar is displayed as a floating toolbar on the screen

5 Click the **Commands** tab if it's not already frontmost

6 Drag buttons to toolbar

Tip:

You can move (or delete) a toolbar button without the Customize dialog box. Just hold down Alt and drag the button to its new location (or drag it off the toolbar altogether to delete it). If you hold down Alt + Ctrl while you drag, the button is copied

5 Click the **Commands** tab

1—4 Create a new toolbar

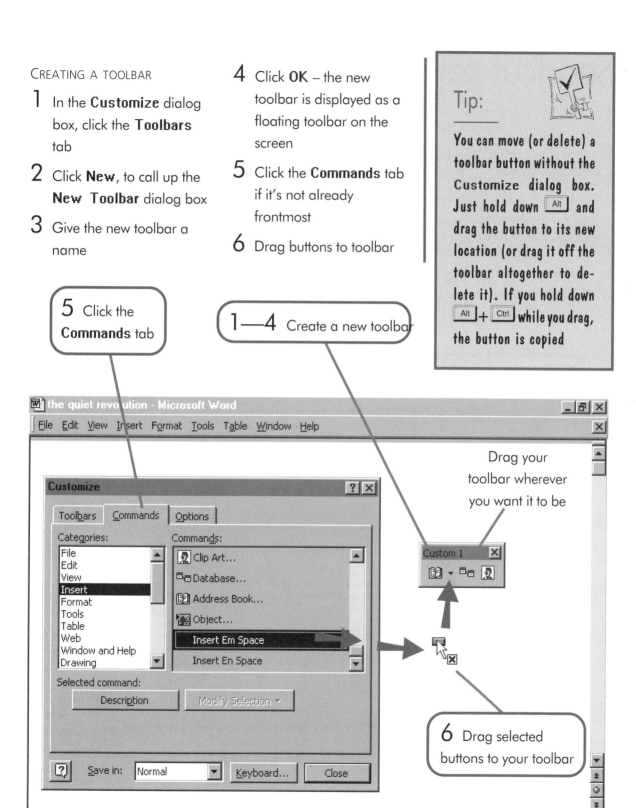

Drag your toolbar wherever you want it to be

6 Drag selected buttons to your toolbar

147

Shortcut keys

A great many things you do in Word, you do a great many times. Some of these things can be called upon with the click of a button on a toolbar, or a shortcut key command. Although buttons are a boon over choosing a command through the ordinary menu method, undoubtedly shortcut keys are the quickest.

At first sight, you might think not all commands are available as shortcuts. However, you can assign your own shortcut key commands to *any* command available in Word.

Basic steps:

1 Choose **Tools↬Customize**, or type `Alt`+`T` then `C`, to call up the **Customize** dialog box (see page 146)

2 Click the **Keyboard** button to display the **Customize Keyboard** dialog box

2 **Customize Keyboard** dialog box

4 Select the command to have a shortcut

3 Select the category of command

9 Click here

5 Enter your new shortcut key here

8 Click here

6 Check to see if the shortcut key is already in use

Description of command selected

Existing shortcuts are displayed here

7 Select the template to save shortcut key in

3 In the **Categories** scrollable list, select the category of the command you want to assign a keyboard shortcut to

4 In the **Commands** scrollable list, locate the command

5 In the **Press new shortcut key** field, enter your desired shortcut. Do this by literally pressing the keys you want as the shortcut

6 View the **Currently assigned to** field directly below the **Press new shortcut key** entry field – Word tells you whether the key is already in use or not. If the shortcut key you want is unassigned you can use it directly. If it's assigned already, you are about to override its previous use. Choose another shortcut key if you want, or go to step 7

7 Locate the template to save your shortcut

8 Click **Assign**

9 Click **Close**

Tip:

You can remove a shortcut key too, by locating the command in the Customize Keyboard dialog box, selecting the shortcut key in the Current keys field, then clicking the Remove button

Tip:

If you save a shortcut key in the default template (Normal.dot) it will be available in *all* new documents you create. If you save it in a *specific* template, on the other hand, it will be available only in new documents you create using that specific template

Tip:

You can revert back to Word's default shortcut key arrangement by clicking the Reset All button on the Customize Keyboard dialog box. Bear in mind though, that this reverts *all* shortcut key changes you have made

Summary

❑ Before printing, preview your work in Print preview. This way you save some paper finding out where your overall problems are.

❑ Use the **Print** dialog box to adjust controls regarding the pages you print, the number of copies you want, and so on.

❑ Use the **Printing options** dialog box to adjust finer details of printing.

❑ Use the Print button 🖨 to print without any dialog boxes.

❑ Start up Word automatically each time you turn on your computer by copying Word's icon to the **StartUp** folder in the Explorer window for the 🏁 Start menu's **Programs** folder.

❑ Adapt existing toolbars, and create your own toolbars, through the **Customize** dialog box, with the **Toolbars** tab frontmost.

❑ Assign your own shortcut keys to commands you use a lot through the **Customize Keyboard** dialog box.

Index

Text formatting
  keyboard shortcuts 49
Toolbars 3, 8, 10
  creating, modifying 146
  default 10
  Tables & Borders 64
Tools menu 5
ToolTips 6
TrueType 47
Typographical symbols 40

U

Undo 35

V

View menu 4
Views
  normal 12
  outline 15
  print layout 14
  Web layout 13

W

Web layout view 13
Widow 56
Window menu 5
Word count 111
WordPerfect users help 27
WYSIWYG 14

Z

Zooming 17